# RICHARD ROHR

# The Universal Christ

HOW A FORGOTTEN REALITY CAN CHANGE
EVERYTHING WE SEE, HOPE FOR,
AND BELIEVE

## Companion Guide for Groups

CAC Publishing
Center for Action and Contemplation
cac.org

CAC PUBLISHING

*Group Guide for The Universal Christ:*
*How a Forgotten Reality Can Change Everything We See, Hope For, and Believe*

Copyright © 2019 Center for Action and Contemplation

Requests for information should be addressed to:

CAC Publishing, PO Box 12464, Albuquerque, New Mexico 87195

ISBN: 978-1-62305-045-0

Scripture citations are Richard Rohr's paraphrase except where noted.

All rights reserved. No part of this publication may be reproduced, stored in a retrieval system, or transmitted in any form or by any means—electronic, mechanical, photocopy, recording, or any other—except for brief quotations in printed reviews, without prior permission of the publisher.

Cover and Interior Design: Nelson Kane
Trinity Tree photograph on page 21 by Nicholas Kramer

First Printing February 2019 / Printed in the United States of America

# ACKNOWLEDGMENTS

This *Companion Guide for Groups* was envisioned by Kirsten Oates, Managing Director of Program Design and Teacher Relations for the Center for Action and Contemplation. She collaborated closely with CAC consultant Patrick Boland, Executive and Leadership Coach for Conexus in Dublin, Ireland, on writing this in-depth, well-crafted guide. Both Kirsten and Patrick are incredibly passionate about *The Universal Christ* and its message.

Vanessa Guerin, Director of Publications for the CAC, and her associate editor, Shirin McArthur, former CAC staff member and founder of Communication Clarified, spent many hours editing this *Companion Guide* in collaboration with Kirsten and Patrick.

I am grateful for their generous efforts in support of my message. Through this *Companion Guide*, I trust that my teaching on the Universal Christ will be experienced more fully by each of you.

—Richard Rohr

# CONTENTS

WHICH GROUP GUIDE SHOULD I CHOOSE?
**7**

INSIGHT GROUP GUIDE
**9**

EMBODIMENT GROUP GUIDE
**61**

ENGAGEMENT GROUP GUIDE
**111**

FACILITATOR GUIDE
**163**

# Which Group Guide Should I Choose?

Thank you for your willingness to participate in a practice group for *The Universal Christ: How a Forgotten Reality Can Change Everything We See, Hope For, and Believe*, Fr. Richard Rohr's most important book to date.

The book and three corresponding Group Guides offer numerous group growth opportunities, including:

- learning about a forgotten teaching on Christ that can impact everything we see, hope for, and believe;
- experiencing the opportunity to learn and engage in Christian contemplative practices;
- participating in a community whose members are growing in their presence to one another; and
- setting intentions for becoming a more loving, engaged presence in the world.

These three Group Guides build on Fr. Richard's teachings in the book. The descriptions below are designed to help determine which group guide will be most appropriate, based on the level of the group's knowledge of Fr. Richard's work. *If the group contains a mix of people at different levels, the Insight Guide is recommended.*

**Insight:** This Group Guide is tailored to people who are new to Fr. Richard's work and the Christian contemplative tradition. There is more time for sharing and a greater level of instruction for the practices. The outcomes for this group include insight into a previously forgotten teaching on Christ and utilizing contemplative practice as a tool for a deeper way of being.

**Embodiment:** This Group Guide is tailored to people who are familiar with both Fr. Richard's work and at least one Christian contemplative practice. The outcomes for this group include recognizing the impact of this teaching on Christ upon day-to-day experiences and the role of contemplative practice as a tool for a deeper way of being.

**Engagement:** This Group Guide is tailored to people who share a deeper resonance with the concepts Fr. Richard teaches and have significant experience with a regular Christian contemplative practice. There is a greater focus on how to engage these concepts to impact the world. The outcomes for this group include committing to new ways of engaging in the world by understanding the critical quality of their presence in shaping community.

A comprehensive Facilitator Guide follows the three Group Guides. These guides have been designed to make the role of facilitator as efficient as possible.

# INSIGHT

Group Guide

Welcome to this Insight practice group for *The Universal Christ: How a Forgotten Reality Can Change Everything We See, Hope For, and Believe*, Fr. Richard Rohr's most important book to date. This Group Guide provides instructions for each practice group session. There will also be a facilitator for your group, who will explain the practices, keep time, guide group sharing, and answer questions you may have about the group process and practices.

Before the first gathering, please read and commit to the following.

## Agreements for Group Participation

- Reading the book.
- Respecting the group guidelines and the role of the facilitator.
- No commenting or interrupting when a group member is sharing.
- Holding confidentiality throughout the course of the group sessions, inside and outside of the sessions.
- Sharing *only* one's own personal story.

## Modalities for Participation

The Group Guide has been formulated in a way that allows for a balance of group work, pair sharing, and solo reflection:

- **Group Work** involves group sharing in a circle using a "talking stick" (introduced by the facilitator at the first session), reflective *Lectio* practice, and contemplative sit. It is a time to deepen into a felt sense of the mind and body of Christ.
- **Pair Sharing** will give individuals an opportunity to share what is true for them with one other person and to practice being an attentive listening presence to their partners.

- **Solo Reflection** is time for individuals to process the content as it relates to their own lives.

## Group Sharing Guidelines

- Gather in a circle.
- Use the talking stick.
- Speak in the moment (try not to prepare something in advance).
- Speak from the heart (speak what is *true* for you, regardless of whether it is "right").
- Be lean of speech (share a few sentences at most, with time to pause and ponder in between).
- Listen from the heart (respect the honest sharing of others and listen in a way that moves you beyond thinking of what this means to *you*; instead, what does this mean to the person who is sharing?).
- Respect confidentiality (what is shared in the group *must* stay in the group; otherwise the group cannot grow together).

In group sharing, be mindful of not speaking or commenting when individuals are sharing. Practicing patience, by not speaking too much and listening in silence, is an important part of group sessions. Each week, bring your copy of *The Universal Christ*, this Group Guide, a journal for recording your reflections, and a Bible to the session.

*Before the first session, read chapters 1 and 2 of* The Universal Christ.

# INSIGHT

**WEEK I OF VIII**
**Chapters: 1 and 2**

**Pair Sharing:**
Before you begin: Reflect for one minute on your thoughts about this concept/request, and how you might commit to participating in this practice group. Share with your partner for two minutes each.

> "You must allow some of the words in this book to *remain partially mysterious, at least for a while*. I know this can be dissatisfying and unsettling to our egoic mind, which wants to be in control every step of the way. Yet this is precisely the contemplative way of reading and listening, and thus being drawn forward into a much Larger Field." (page 6)

When it's your turn to listen, do not ask questions, interrupt, or interject in any way. Allow for silence and simply thank your partner for sharing. This paired exercise is simply to listen to each other.

**Solo Reflection:**

> "[Seeing] Christ as ubiquitous and eternal . . . [is] somewhat of a reclamation project. . . . What if Christ is *another name for everything*—in its fullness?" (pages 4, 5)

Take three minutes to read at least one of the referenced Scriptures (Colossians 1, Ephesians 1, John 1, Hebrews 1) and write a few words in your journal that summarize how *you* experience the Resurrected Christ in the world today.

**Group Sharing (with Talking Stick):**
Take two minutes to silently reflect on this quotation:

> "A merely personal God becomes tribal and sentimental, and a merely universal God never leaves the realm of abstract theory and philosophical principles.... together, Jesus and Christ give us a God who is both *personal* and *universal*." (page 19)

Your facilitator will review the Group Sharing Guidelines. Then you will take turns sharing your thoughts with the group. (Twenty minutes total are allocated for this round of group sharing.)

**Solo Reflection:**
Take two minutes to read this quotation and reflect on the two questions in your journal.

> "[Jesus] says it is those who 'do it right' that matter, not those who 'say it right.' Yet verbal orthodoxy has been Christianity's preoccupation, at times even allowing us to burn people at the stake for not 'saying it right.' This is what happens when we focus solely on an exclusive Jesus, on having a 'personal relationship' with him, and on what he can do to save you and me from some eternal, fiery torment. For the first two thousand years of Christianity, we framed our faith in terms of a problem and a threat." (pages 17–18)

What are the first thoughts that come to mind when you read this?

How do you feel, on an emotional and a physical level, as you reflect on this?

**Pair Sharing:**
In pairs, take five minutes total to reflect on the contrasts between the following two quotations from chapter 2 and share what arises for you with your partner.

> "As long as we keep God imprisoned in a retributive frame instead of a restorative frame, we really have no substantial good news; it

is neither good nor new, but the same old tired story line of history. We pull God down to our level." (pages 28–29)

"Building on 2 Peter 1:4, where the author says, 'He has given us something very great and wonderful . . . you are *able to share the divine nature!*' This is Christianity's core good news and only transformative message." (pages 27–28)

**Group Sharing (with Talking Stick):**
*Lectio* Introductory Exercise. (Twenty minutes total are allocated for this round of group sharing.)

**FACILITATOR:**

*Introduces* this first *Lectio* by reading the following:

*"Contemplation is waiting patiently for the gaps to be filled in, and it does not insist on quick closure or easy answers.* It never rushes to judgment and in fact avoids making quick judgments because judgments have more to do with egoic, personal control than with a loving search for truth." (page 8) (Pause)

"Sit with each italicized sentence and, if need be, read it again until you feel its impact, until . . . 'the word becomes flesh' for you!" (page 8) (Pause)

"Have you ever noticed that the expression 'the light of the world' is used to describe the Christ (John 8:12), but that Jesus also applies the same phrase to us? (Matthew 5:14, 'You are the light of the world.') Few preachers ever pointed that out to me." (page 31) (Pause)

The text for our *Lectio* is Matthew 5:14: "You are the light of the world." (Pause)

***Reads*** the text slowly and clearly for the whole group to hear. Group members may read along with the text or choose to close their eyes and simply listen. (This first reading is to help group members familiarize themselves with the quotation.)

***Reads*** the text slowly and clearly a second time. Each person allows the quotation to "wash over them," noticing which word or phrase stands out for them.

After a few moments of silence, one person picks up the talking stick and briefly shares the word or phrase that stood out for them (the word or phrase that encapsulates their divine lesson). Then, passing the talking stick around the circle, everyone takes a turn to briefly share the word or phrase that stood out for them. If anyone chooses not to share a word or phrase, they simply say "pass" and hand the talking stick to the next person.

### Solo Reflection:
In silence, take one minute to linger over this word or phrase; "to focus on it until it engages your body, your heart, your awareness of the physical [and unseen] world around you." (page 8)

**FACILITATOR:**

***Invites*** each person to take the talking stick and share, in just a few sentences, the connection between the word or phrase and their life.

***Reads*** the passage one last time and invites the group to sit in contemplative silence for two minutes, allowing the divine lesson to sink in and settle within their whole being.

***Closes*** the group with the bell and invites people to leave in silence.

## Solo Reflection at Home (Optional):

### Exercise 1

> "Have you ever noticed that the expression 'the light of the world' is used to describe the Christ (John 8:12), but that Jesus also applies the same phrase to us? (Matthew 5:14, 'You are the light of the world.') Few preachers ever pointed that out to me." (page 31)

> "For you who have felt angered or wounded or excluded by the message of Jesus or Christ as you have heard it, I hope you sense an opening here—an affirmation, a welcome that you may have despaired of ever hearing." (page 36)

Mull over these two quotations throughout the week and, when you feel ready, record your reflections in your journal. (These reflections will not be shared with the group.)

### Exercise 2

On your own, practice *Lectio* with the text, "You are the light of the world" (Matthew 5:14) using the format from this week's session.

*Please read chapters 3 and 4 before our next meeting.*

## WEEK II OF VIII
**Chapters: 3 and 4**

**FACILITATOR:**

*Invites* the group to get comfortable, take some deep breaths, let go of the stresses of the day, and sit in silence for one minute.

**Solo Reflection:**
Spend two minutes pondering these quotations and questions in your journal.

> "He does not say 'God revealed his Son *to* me' as you might expect. Instead, he says, 'God revealed his Son *in* me' (Galatians 1:16)." (pages 40–41)

> *"When you can honor and receive your own moment of sadness or fullness as a gracious participation in the eternal sadness or fullness of God, you are beginning to recognize yourself as a participating member of this one universal Body. You are moving from I to We."* (page 42)

How have you experienced this participation in the eternal sadness or fullness of God?

Reflect on the idea that this experience means you are "a participating member of this one universal Body." If helpful, record any thoughts, images, or emotions that this brings up for you.

**Pair Sharing:**
Read the following quotations silently:

> "'There is only Christ. He is everything and he is in everything' (Colossians 3:11)." (page 43)

> "Paul calls this bigger Divine identity the 'mystery of his purpose, the hidden plan he so kindly made *en Cristo* from the very beginning' (Ephesians 1:9). Today, we might call it the 'collective unconscious.'" (page 44)

Then, one of the pair slowly reads the following quotation out loud, repeating it twice more to let the words sink in:

> *"I have never been separate from God, nor can I be, except in my mind."* (page 44)

Share your responses to the following for two minutes each:

As you listened to the above quotation, what arose for you:

> On a cognitive level? (Thoughts)
> On an emotional level? (Feelings)
> On a physiological level? (Sensations)

**Group Sharing (with Talking Stick):**

> "Without a Shared and Big Story, we all retreat into private individualism for a bit of sanity and safety. Perhaps the primary example of our lack of attention to the Christ Mystery can be seen in the way we continue to pollute and ravage planet earth, the very thing we all stand on and live from. Science now appears to love and respect physicality more than most religion does! No wonder that *science and business have taken over as the major explainers of meaning* for the vast majority of people today (even many who still go to church). We Christians did not take this world seriously, I am afraid, because our notion of God or salvation didn't include or honor the physical universe. And now, I am afraid, the world does not take us seriously." (page 46)

Take two minutes to reflect on this quote in silence. Then use the talking stick to share your thoughts with the group. (Twenty minutes total are allocated for this round of group sharing.) (Your facilitator will remind you of the talking stick guidelines.)

**Solo Reflection:**
Spend two minutes pondering these quotations and questions in your journal.

> "Just because you do not have the right word for God does not mean you are not having the right experience." (page 51)

> "Any kind of authentic God experience will usually feel like love or suffering, or both. It will connect you to Full Reality at ever-new breadths, and depths 'until God will be all in all' (1 Corinthians 15:28). Our circles of belonging tend to either expand or constrict as life goes on." (page 51)

Has your faith life been more concerned with having "the right word for God" or having "the right experience"? How has this affected you?

Are the circles of belonging expanding or constricting in your life right now?

**Pair Sharing:**

> "Do we really think that God had nothing at all to say for 13.7 billion years, and started speaking only in the latest nanosecond of geological time? Did all history prior to our sacred texts provide no basis for truth or authority? Of course not. . . . But in the mid-nineteenth century, grasping for the certitude and authority the church was quickly losing in the face of rationalism and scientism, Catholics declared the Pope to be 'infallible,' and Evangelicals decided the Bible was 'inerrant,' despite the fact that we had gotten along for most of eighteen hundred

years without either belief. In fact, these claims would have seemed idolatrous to most early Christians." (page 58)

"After Augustine, most Christian theologies shifted from the positive vision of Genesis 1 to the darker vision of Genesis 3—the so-called fall, or what I am calling the 'problem.' Instead of embracing God's master plan for humanity and creation . . . Christians shrunk our image of both Jesus and Christ, and our 'Savior' became a mere Johnny-come-lately 'answer' to the problem of sin, a problem that we had largely created ourselves." (page 61)

What stands out for you the most in these quotations? In pairs, take turns sharing for four minutes each. When it's your turn to listen, do not ask questions, interrupt, or interject in any way. Allow for silence and simply thank your partner for sharing. This paired exercise is simply to listen to each other.

**FACILITATOR:**

Thank you for sharing in pairs. We are now going to practice the spiritual discipline of silence by doing a contemplative sit. The theme for our sit, as illustrated in the photograph of the cottonwood tree, is:

> "*Divine perfection is precisely the ability to include what seems like imperfection.*" (page 55) (Pause)

As we begin our sit, let's take a few moments to notice our posture. Becoming comfortable in our seat, let's sit slightly forward, so that our spine is no longer touching the back of the seat. (Pause) Let's become aware of both of our feet touching the floor, grounding us in the present moment. (Pause) Let's focus on our back and our neck, allowing them to find their most aligned and neutral positions. (Pause) Now, I invite us to lower our gaze and focus on a point on the floor in front of us. Or, if we feel comfortable, we may want to close our eyes. (Pause)

As we begin our contemplation, let's remember that we are not trying to "achieve" anything. (Pause) There are no goals. (Pause) We are simply becoming aware of this moment. (Pause) Becoming aware of our presence in this moment. (Pause) Noticing any distractions, thoughts, judgments, decisions, ideas that cross our mind, we choose to let them go for now (Pause) and to focus instead on our moment-by-moment experience of being present to What Is. (Pause) God's Presence (Pause); the Larger Field (Pause); *en Cristo* (Pause). As we become distracted, frustrated, or confused, we consciously return to offering up our moment-by-moment presence to God's Presence by using a sacred word, such as Yah-weh or Je-sus, or simply focus on our breath—in and out—whenever distracting thoughts enter our minds. (Pause) We know that God's Presence is already within us, whether we're aware of it or not. (Pause) No offering up is needed—we are offering in. (Pause) Into the silence. (Pause) Into each moment that we sit in contemplation. (Pause)

**Reads** the text slowly and clearly for the whole group to hear: "*Divine perfection is precisely the ability to include what seems like imperfection.*" (Pause)

*Rings* a prayer bell to indicate that the contemplative sit has begun.

*After* ten minutes, the facilitator rings a prayer bell to indicate that the contemplative sit has finished.

*Invites* sharing: "Since this was our first time practicing a contemplative sit together, take turns sharing the experience with the person beside you for two minutes each."

*Closes* the group with the bell and invites people to leave in silence.

### Solo Reflection at Home (Optional):

### Exercise 1

> "Along with *en Cristo,* Paul loves to use words like 'wisdom,' 'secret,' 'hidden plan,' and 'mystery.' . . . the direct meaning of Paul's *secret mystery* is the Christ we are talking about in this book." (page 49)

Read one or more of the Pauline Epistles and notice where and when the words "wisdom," "secret," "hidden plan," and "mystery" are mentioned. How does this reading affect your understanding of what Paul is saying?

What impact does this have on you?

### Exercise 2

> *"How you do anything is how you do everything."* (page 57)

Leading in with this quotation, practice a contemplative sit of your own this week.

Seat yourself in a quiet area.

Ground yourself and allow your breathing to settle.

Notice any tightness in your shoulders and neck and allow any tension in your muscles to relax.

Allow your back to rest in an aligned, neutral position.

Once you are settled, read the passage aloud—this is the opening text for your sit.

Continue in your sit in whatever way makes most sense to you—focusing on your breath, connecting with your body, or another method with which you are familiar from group contemplative sits or your own experience of contemplative practice.

You may wish to set a timer or a prayer bell so that you know when to finish.

Remember, there is no goal; there is no right or wrong way—simply *be* present to what *is* in the moment.

Write in your journal your reflections of your experience of this sit.

*Please read chapters 5, 6, and 7 before our next meeting.*

## WEEK III OF VIII
Chapters: 5 through 7

*Lectio*

**FACILITATOR:**

*Welcomes* the group and invites everyone to observe a minute of silence by way of settling into their seats and feeling present to themselves and the rest of the group.

*States* that the text for the *Lectio* is from chapter 5 and reads the text slowly and clearly for the whole group to hear. Group members may read along with the text or choose to close their eyes and simply listen. (This first reading is to help the group familiarize themselves with the quotation.)

> "The Crucified and Risen Christ uses the mistakes of the past to create a positive future, a future of redemption instead of retribution. He does not eliminate or punish the mistakes. He uses them for transformative purposes. People formed by such love are indestructible. Forgiveness might just be the very best description of what God's goodness engenders in humanity." (page 72) (Pause)

*Reads* the passage slowly and clearly a second time. Each person allows the quotation to "wash over them," noticing which word or phrase stands out for them.

### Group Sharing (with Talking Stick):
After a few moments of silence, one person picks up the talking stick and briefly shares the word or phrase that stood out for them. Then, going around in a circle, everyone takes a turn to briefly share the word or phrase that stood out for them. If anyone chooses not to share a word or phrase, they simply say "pass"' and hand the talking

stick to the next person. (Two minutes total are allocated for this round of group sharing.)

## Solo Reflection:
In silence, take one minute to linger over this word or phrase; "to focus on it until it engages your body, your heart, your awareness of the physical [and unseen] world around you." (page 8)

## FACILITATOR:

*Invites* each person to take the talking stick and share, in just a few sentences, the connection between the word or phrase and their life. (Ten minutes total are allocated for this round of group sharing.)

*Reads* the passage one last time. The group sits in contemplative silence for two minutes, allowing the *Lectio* to sink in and settle within their whole being.

## Solo Reflection:
Take two minutes to read this quotation and reflect on the two questions in your journal.

> "After years of counseling both religious and nonreligious people, it seems to me that most humans need a love object (which will then become a subject!) to keep themselves both sane and happy. That love object becomes our 'North Star,' serving as our moral compass and our reason to keep putting one foot in front of the other in a happy and hopeful way. All of us need someone or something to connect our hearts with our heads. Love grounds us by creating focus, direction, motivation, even joy—and if we don't find these things in love, we usually will try to find them in hate." (page 74)

When have you experienced this love object with someone (or something)? What was positive or whole about that experience?

When have you lacked having a love object in your life? How did this affect you?

**Pair Sharing:**

> Jesus refused "to enforce or even bother with what he considered secondary issues like the Sabbath, ritual laws, purity codes, membership requirements, debt codes, on and on. He saw they were only 'human commandments,' which far too often took the place of love." (page 73)

In pairs, reflect for two minutes each on the "membership requirements" and experiences of "human commandments" that have been formative in your early stage religious experiences.

> What experiences helped you and your spiritual development?
> What experiences hindered you and your spiritual development?

**Group Sharing (with Talking Stick):**
Take one minute to reflect on this passage:

> "Many educated and sophisticated people are not willing to submit to indirect, subversive, and intuitive knowing, which is probably why they rely far too much on external law and ritual behavior to achieve their spiritual purposes." (pages 85–86)

Use the talking stick to share your thoughts on this with the group. (Eight minutes total are allocated for this round of group sharing.) (Your facilitator will remind you of the talking stick guidelines.)

**Solo Reflection:**
Take five minutes to read this quotation and reflect on the questions in your journal.

"How does anyone achieve such a holding together of opposites—things like inner acceptance and outer resistance, intense suffering and perfect freedom, my little self and an infinite God, sensuality and intense spirituality, the need to blame somebody and the freedom to blame nobody?... Christ [is] a universally available 'voice' that calls all things to *become whole and true to themselves*. God's two main tools in this direction, from every appearance, seem to be great love and great suffering—and often great love that *invariably leads* to great suffering." (page 83)

Reflect on a time in your life when you experienced great love or great suffering. What happened? Who was involved?

What emotions did you feel at that time? Looking back, was there a tension of opposites in the situation (e.g., "intense suffering and perfect freedom")?

Did this experience lead you to become more *"whole and true"* to yourself? If so, in what way(s)? If not, what effect did this experience have on you?

How does this experience continue to influence you today?

**Pair Sharing:**
Begin by silently reading through the quotations and questions below. Then, after two minutes of reflection, take turns asking the questions below the last quote (allow five minutes for each partner to share).

It is important to listen to your partner without interrupting them or asking any questions. Let them answer the questions in their own time, giving them plenty of space for reflection and silence. Resist the temptation to "fix" or interject at all. Your role is to simply listen and to thank them for sharing once they are done.

When your partner is finished speaking, trade places and repeat the process.

> "Jesus quite clearly believed in change. In fact, the first public word out of his mouth was the Greek imperative verb *metanoeite*, which literally translates as "change your mind" or "go beyond your mind" (Matthew 3:2, 4:17, and Mark 1:15). Unfortunately, in the fourth century, St. Jerome translated the word into Latin as *paenitentia* ("repent" or "do penance"), initiating a host of moralistic connotations that have colored Christians' understanding of the Gospels ever since. The word *metanoeite*, however, is talking about *a primal change of mind, worldview, or your way of processing*—and only by corollary about a specific change in behavior." (page 92)

Imagine you were to go back and hear somebody preach the message of the Gospel to you for the first time. Rather than saying "repent and believe the Good News," they quote Jesus as saying, "change your mind about God; change your worldview; change your way of seeing; God is closer than you think." What would your initial reaction to the message of the Gospel have been? (Pause for your partner's response.)

> "I love the image of fire, not for its seeming destructiveness, but as a natural symbol for transformation—literally, the changing of forms. Farmers, forestry workers, and native peoples know that fire is a renewing force, even as it also can be destructive. We in the West tend to see it as merely destructive (which is probably why we did not understand the metaphors of hell or purgatory)." (page 92)

In your life today, what ideas about God, yourself, or the world in which we live need to be "set on fire" and destroyed? Take a moment to sit with this. Go with your instinct. (Pause for your partner's response.)

If the idea was to be "set on fire," what transformation could then take place within you? (Pause for your partner's response.)

**FACILITATOR:**

*Invites* the group to end the session by practicing a contemplative sit. The preparatory text for the sit is a quote from Cardinal John Henry Newman:

> "To live is to change, and to be perfect is to have changed often." (page 97)

*Invites* group members to take a moment to notice their posture; become comfortable in their seat; sit slightly forward, until their spine is no longer touching the back of the seat. (Pause)

Become aware of both feet touching the floor, grounding you in the present moment. (Pause)

Focus on your back and neck. Find your most neutral position, taking a moment to allow your back and neck to align. (Pause)

Lower your gaze and focus on a point on the floor in front of you. Or, close your eyes if that is more comfortable. (Pause)

You are not trying to "achieve" anything (pause); there are no goals (pause); you are simply becoming aware of the moment (pause); becoming aware of your presence in the moment (pause); noticing any distractions, thoughts, judgments, decisions, ideas that cross your mind, choosing to let them go in the moment (pause), and, rather, focusing on your moment-by-moment experience of being present to What Is (pause); God's Presence (pause); the Larger Field (pause); *en Cristo* (pause).

As you become distracted, frustrated, or confused, consciously return to offering up your moment-by-moment presence to God's Presence by using a sacred word or simply focusing on your breath (pause). Then, you realize that God's Presence is already within you, whether you're aware of it or not (pause).

No offering up is needed—you are offering in (pause): Into the silence (pause); into each moment that you sit in contemplation (pause).

***Reads*** the text slowly and clearly for the whole group to hear:

> "To live is to change, and to be perfect is to have changed often." (Pause)

***Rings*** a prayer bell to indicate that the contemplative sit has begun. After five minutes, the facilitator rings a prayer bell to indicate that the contemplative sit has finished, and the session has ended.

### Solo Reflection at Home (Optional):

### Exercise 1

> "As C. G. Jung inscribed over his doorway, *Vocatus atque non vocatus, Deus aderit*, 'Invoked or not invoked, God is still present.'" (page 100)

Write in your journal a few experiences and situations in your week where God was "invoked."

What are these experiences like for you?

Write down an experience in your week where God was "not invoked," but your faith attested to God being present.

What was this experience like for you?

Is there any difference between the two types of experiences? Why or why not?

**Exercise 2**

> "Life does not have to be perfect to be wonderful." (page 97)

Leading in with this quotation, practice another contemplative sit of your own this week. You may wish to set a timer or a prayer bell so that you know when to finish. If you wish, write down your reflections of your experience of this sit.

*Please read chapters 8, 9, and 10 before our next meeting.*

## WEEK IV OF VIII
## Chapters: 8 through 10

**FACILITATOR:**

***Welcomes*** the group and invites everyone to settle into their seats as s/he slowly reads the following:

> "Have you ever noticed the huge leap the creed makes between 'born of the Virgin Mary' and 'suffered under Pontius Pilate'? *A single comma* connects the two statements, and falling into that yawning gap, as if it were a mere detail, is *everything* Jesus said and did between his birth and his death! Called the 'Great Comma.'" (pages 103–104)

***Pauses*** for a moment and then says:

> The Great Comma: everything Jesus said and did between his birth and his death.

***Pauses***, then invites the group to sit in silence for two minutes, saying:

> Focus on your breath in and your breath out as you experience the "fleeting comma" of your own life in these few moments of silence.

## Solo Reflection:
Take five minutes to read these quotations and reflect on the questions in your journal.

> "As I watch Catholics receive communion at Mass, I notice that some, after taking the bread and wine, turn toward the altar or the sacred box that reserves the bread and bow or genuflect as a gesture of respect—as if the Presence were still over there.... Don't

> they realize that the Eucharist was supposed to be a full transference of identity to *them*?" (page 109)

> "I have known many Evangelicals who 'received Jesus into their hearts' but still felt the need to 'get saved' again every Friday night. Did they not believe that a real transformation happened if they made a genuine surrender and reconnected to their Source? Most of us understandably start the journey assuming that God is 'up there,' and our job is to transcend this world to find 'him.'" (page 110)

**Reflecting on these examples, what has been your own experience of God "up there"?**

> "We spend so much time trying to get 'up there,' we miss that God's big leap in Jesus was to come 'down here.'" (page 110)

Given your current experience of faith and spirituality, where is God for you right now: "up there," "down here," or elsewhere? (This reflection will not be shared with anyone, so go with your gut instinct, avoiding any temptation to write the "correct" response.)

**Pair Sharing:**
In pairs, share which aspect(s) of the quotation below make(s) most sense to you. What from your own life experience has influenced this? (Allow three minutes for each person.)

> "Humanity now needs a Jesus who is historical, relevant for real life, physical and concrete, like we are. A Jesus whose life can save you even more than his death. A Jesus we can practically imitate, and who sets the bar for what it means to be fully human. And a Christ who is big enough to hold all creation together in one harmonious unity." (page 107)

## Group Sharing (with Talking Stick):

**FACILITATOR:**

***Reminds*** the group to use the talking stick to share their reflections with the group. Invites members to read the quotations below.

> "Remember, the archetypal encounter between doubting Thomas and the Risen Jesus (John 20:19–28) is not really a story about believing in the fact of the resurrection, but a story about believing that someone could *be wounded and also resurrected at the same time!* . . . 'Put your finger here,' Jesus says to Thomas (20:27). And, like Thomas, we are indeed wounded and resurrected at the same time, all of us. In fact, this might be the primary pastoral message of the whole Gospel." (page 111)

> "We cannot jump over this world, or its woundedness, and still try to love God. We must love God *through, in, with,* and even *because of* this world." (page 112)

Take a minute to reflect on these quotations and relate them to your own life. Do you have experience of being "wounded and resurrected at the same time"? Each member is invited to share with the group, using the talking stick. (Fifteen minutes total are allocated for this round of group sharing.)

## Solo Reflection:
Take three minutes to read this quotation and reflect on the questions in your journal.

> "We were made to love and trust this world, 'to cultivate it and take care of it' (Genesis 2:15), but for some sad reason we preferred to emphasize the statement that comes three verses later, which seems to say that we should 'dominate' the earth (1:28), where

within one generation we become killers of our brothers (Genesis 4:8)." (pages 112–113)

In what ways have you loved and trusted this world?

In what ways have you sought to dominate or enforce your own way in the world?

What have been the repercussions of both approaches, in your own life and in the lives of those around you?

**Pair Sharing:**

> "I doubt if you can see the image of God (*Imago Dei*) in your fellow humans if you cannot first see it in rudimentary form in stones, in plants and flowers, in strange little animals, in bread and wine, and most especially cannot honor this objective divine image in yourself. It is a full-body tune-up, this spiritual journey. It really ends up being *all or nothing, here and then everywhere*." (page 119)

Taking turns with your partner (for five minutes each), reflect on a moment when you saw the image of God in stones, plants, flowers, bread and wine, or within yourself. Describe what happened and the sense you experienced. What did you feel, see, say, taste, and hear? How did this "seeing" affect your view of your "fellow humans"?

**Group Sharing (with Talking Stick):**
Take one minute to reflect on these quotations.

> "The point is that in some ways, many humans can identify with Mary more than they can with Jesus precisely because she was *not* God, but the archetype for our yes to God! Not one heroic action is attributed to her, only trust itself. *Pure being and not doing*." (page 127)

*"Mary is all of us both receiving and handing on the gift."* (page 124)

Use the talking stick to share your thoughts with the group. (Fifteen minutes total are allocated for this round of group sharing.)

Facilitator closes the group with the bell and invites people to leave in silence.

**Solo Reflection at Home (Optional):**

**Exercise 1**

> "In Mary, humanity has said *our* eternal yes to God. A yes that cannot be undone. A corporate yes that overrides our many noes." (page 128)

Notice and write in your journal the times and situations in your week where you are answering God or life with a no (for some, this might even include a no to relating your home reflection to Mary).

Notice and write in your journal the times and situations in your week where you are answering God or life with a yes.

Where in your life *would* you like to answer God with a yes? Meditate on this (or even pray for this) in whatever way seems most fitting to you.

*Please read chapters 11 and 12 before our next meeting.*

# WEEK V OF VIII
## Chapters: 11 and 12

**FACILITATOR:**

*Reads* the following quotation:

> "Life is the destiny you are bound to refuse until you have consented to die."
> —W. H. Auden, "For the Time Being" (page 129)

*Invites* the group to get comfortable, take some deep breaths, let go of the stresses of the day, and sit in silence for one minute. (The facilitator may choose to use a prayer bell to mark the opening and closing of this short, one-minute sit.)

*Reads* the quotation again, waits for another minute, then invites participants into solo reflection.

## Solo Reflection:
Spend two minutes pondering the quotation and questions in your journal.

> "When Jesus spoke the words 'This is my Body,' I believe he was speaking not just about the bread right in front of him, but about the whole universe, about everything that is physical, material, and yet also spirit-filled. . . . The bread and wine, and all of creation, seem to believe who and what they are much more readily than humans do. They know they are the Body of Christ, even if the rest of us resist such a thought." (pages 131–132)

Take a moment to examine your own hands. Do you know that your hands and your entire physical body "are the Body of Christ"? Write down any thoughts, questions, or images that come to you.

"The bread and wine, and all of creation, seem to believe who and what they are much more readily than humans do." Write down any thoughts, questions, or images that come to you.

**Pair Sharing:**

> "We must keep eating and drinking the Mystery, until one day it dawns on us, in an undefended moment, 'My God, I really am what I eat! I also am the Body of Christ.'" (page 136)

> "The bread and wine are largely understood as *an exclusive presence*, when in fact their full function is to communicate a truly inclusive—and always shocking—presence." (page 134)

In pairs, take two minutes each to share which aspect(s) of the above quotations resonate with you. If you'd prefer, you may instead share some of your reflections from the solo exercise above.

**Group Sharing (with Talking Stick):**
Take a minute to reflect on these quotations:

> "Thinking he could solve the problem of sin inside of the medieval code of feudal honor and shame, Anselm said, in effect, 'Yes, a price did need to be paid to restore God's honor, and it needed to be paid to God the Father—by one who was equally divine.' . . . In authoritarian and patriarchal cultures, most people were fully programmed to think this way. . . . [T]his understanding also nullifies any in-depth spiritual journey: *Why would you love or trust or desire to be with such a God?*" (page 143)

> "Over the next few centuries, Anselm's honor- and shame-based way of thinking came to be accepted among Christians, though it met resistance from some, particularly my own Franciscan school. Protestants accepted the mainline Catholic position and embraced

it with even more fervor. Evangelicals later enshrined it as one of the 'four pillars' of foundational Christian belief, which the earlier period would have thought strange." (page 143)

Decide what you may want to share with the group; is your focus primarily on the ideas and theology of shame-based thinking, or is it primarily on your personal experience of shame-based thinking? Using the talking stick, share with the group. (Fifteen minutes total are allocated for this round of group sharing.)

As you listen to others, notice what thoughts and emotions arise within you. As you do this, please do not debate, defend, or disagree with others while they speak, or when it is your turn to speak.

**Solo Reflection:**

> "*It is not God who is violent. We are.*
> *It is not that God demands suffering of humans. We do.*
> *God does not need or want suffering—neither in Jesus nor in us.*"
> (page 146)

Sit with this quotation for one minute, then spend a minute journaling anything that comes up for you.

**Pair Sharing:**
Take two minutes to read through the following quotations silently and notice what resonates with you.

> "The Divine Mind transforms all human suffering by identifying completely with the human predicament and standing in full solidarity with it from beginning to end. This is the real meaning of the crucifixion. The cross is not just a singular event. It's a statement from God that *reality has a cruciform pattern*." (page 147)

> *"There is a science about which God knows nothing—addition and subtraction."*
> —Thérèse of Lisieux (page 147)

> "If we do not recognize that we ourselves are the problem, we will continue to make God the scapegoat—which is exactly what we did by the killing of the God-Man on the cross. The crucifixion of Jesus—whom we see as the Son of God—was a devastating prophecy that humans would sooner kill God than change themselves. Yet the God-Man suffers our rejection willingly so something bigger can happen." (page 154)

Now, with your partner, take turns sharing what resonated for you, for two minutes each.

**FACILITATOR:**

*Reads* the text below for the *Lectio*, slowly and clearly for the whole group to hear. Group members may read along with the text or choose to close their eyes and simply listen.

> *"He did not come to change God's mind about us. It did not need changing. Jesus came to change our minds about God—and about ourselves—and about where goodness and evil really lie."* (page 151) (Pause)

*Reads* the passage slowly and clearly a second time. Each person allows the quotation to "wash over them," noticing which word or phrase stands out for them.

### Group Sharing (with Talking Stick):
After one minute of silence, one person picks up the talking stick and briefly shares the word or phrase that stood out for them. Then, going around in a circle, everyone takes a turn to briefly share the word or phrase that stood out for them. If anyone chooses not to

share a word or phrase, they simply say "pass" and hand the talking stick to the next person. (Two minutes total are allocated for this round of group sharing.)

**Solo Reflection:**
In silence, take one minute to linger over this word or phrase; "to focus on it until it engages your body, your heart, your awareness of the physical [and unseen] world around you." (page 8)

**FACILITATOR:**

*Invites* each person to take the talking stick and share, in a few sentences, the connection between the word or phrase and their life. (Fifteen minutes total are allocated for this round of group sharing.)

*Reads* the passage one last time and the group sits in contemplative silence for five minutes, allowing the divine lesson to sink in and settle within their whole being.

*Closes* the group with the bell and invites people to leave in silence.

**Solo Reflection at Home (Optional):**

**Exercise 1**

Using the text from the Group *Lectio*, do your own *Lectio* at home:

> "He did not come to change God's mind about us. It did not need changing. Jesus came to change our minds about God—and about ourselves—and about where goodness and evil really lie."

The next day, use this text as the introduction to a contemplative sit:

"[You] are the Body of Christ." (page 132)

You may want to practice this *Lectio* and this sit more than once during the week.

**Exercise 2**

"A Dialogue with the Crucified God"

"Wait until you have an open, quiet, and solitary slot of time, then pray it out loud so your ears can hear your own words from your own mouth. In addition, I suggest that you place yourself before a tender image of the crucified Jesus that will allow you to both give and receive." (page 155)

Following the instructions above, read through "A Dialogue with the Crucified God" (pages 155–158) at some point this week. Journal anything that arises for you.

*Please read chapters 13, 14, and 15 before our next meeting.*

**WEEK VI OF VIII**
**Chapters: 13 through 15**

**FACILITATOR:**

***Welcomes*** the group and invites everyone to a minute of silence by way of settling into their seats and feeling present to themselves and the rest of the group, then slowly reads the following:

> "Almost all people are carrying a great and secret hurt, even when they don't know it." (page 161)

***Pauses*** for a moment and then invites group members to notice what comes up for them as they hear the quote one more time. Then the group will take two minutes of silence. Members may want to reflect on this quote or simply sit in the silence and connect with their body, noticing how they are feeling and any sensations that they may be experiencing.

***Slowly reads*** the quotation one last time and then gives the group two minutes to sit in silence:

> "Almost all people are carrying a great and secret hurt, even when they don't know it."

**Solo Reflection:**
Take three minutes to reflect on the quotation that your facilitator read to begin the session, as well as the quotation below, and respond to the following questions in your journal. (You will not be asked to share your responses.)

> "The only way out of deep sadness is to go *with it* and *through it*.... When I try to heroically do it alone, I slip into distractions, denials, and pretending—and *I do not learn suffering's softening lessons.*" (page 161)

What is coming up for you as you reflect on these quotations?

What has been your experience of "deep sadness"? Have you gone through it alone and slipped into distractions, denials, or pretending?

What is it like, or what *would* it be like, "to go *with it* and *through it*"? Is there someone in your life that could support you?

**Pair Sharing:**
In pairs, take two minutes each to talk about the aspects of this quotation that resonate with you and your life experience:

> "One side effect of our individualized reading of the Gospel is that it allows the clergy great control over individual behavior, via threats and rewards. Obedience to authorities became the highest virtue in this framework, instead of love, communion, or solidarity with God or others, including the marginalized." (page 165)

When it's your turn to listen, do not ask questions, interrupt, or interject in any way. Allow for silence. This paired exercise is simply to listen to each other.

**Group Sharing (with Talking Stick):**

> *"'Resurrection' is another word for change, but particularly positive change—which we tend to see only in the long run. In the short run, it often just looks like death.* The Preface to the Catholic funeral liturgy says, 'Life is not ended, it is merely changed.'" (pages 170–171)

Take two minutes to reflect in silence on your experience of loss and pain, of resurrection and new beginnings. This may relate to a personal challenge you have had, the ending of a friendship/relationship, or any other life event that strongly impacted you. What was this experience like for you? (Take care of yourself by choosing something you can talk about without feeling overwhelmed in front of the group.)

Group members take turns with the talking stick. As you take hold of the talking stick, start off by saying: "Life is not ended, it is merely changed." Then, trust your instinct to say whatever arises within you in that moment—even if it is different than what you had been thinking about beforehand. (Fifteen minutes total are allocated for this round of group sharing.)

**Solo Reflection:**
Take five minutes to reflect on these quotations and questions in your journal.

> "To negatively connect, to hate, fear, or oppose, is *not* to meet the Divine Personality. Thus we are strongly warned against such negativity in every way, and such things are called 'sin' or even the state of 'hell,' which is not really a geographical place but a very real state of consciousness. All rewards and punishments must primarily be seen as first of all *now—and inherent in good and bad behavior.* (page 175)

Where are you negatively connecting, hating, fearing, or opposing in your life right now?

Describe what this feels like on a day-to-day/week-to-week basis.

> "It is very interesting to me that the New Testament only 'sends out' those (*apostolos*) who can be 'witnesses to resurrection' (Luke 24:48, Acts 1:22, 3:15b, 13:31), that is, witnesses to this immense inner and outer conversation that is always going on. Otherwise, we have little to say that is really helpful, and we just create unnecessary problems for people. Negative or cynical people, conspiracy theorists, and all predictors of Armageddon are the polar

> opposites of witnesses to resurrection. And many such people appear to be running the world and even the churches. The Christ of John's Gospel says, 'Be brave. I have overcome the world' (16:33) and its hopelessness. Courage and confidence is our message! Not threat and fear." (pages 175–176)

Focusing on the final quote, from John's Gospel, write down the first thoughts, feelings, sensations, or images that come to you.

> *"If you are frightened into God, it is never the true God that you meet. If you are loved into God, you meet a God worthy of both Jesus and Christ. How you get there is where you arrive."* (page 181)

How did *you* get there? Where have you arrived today?

**Pair Sharing:**

> "The first apostle was a woman. And saying that is not trying to be politically correct. It's true by the early definition of an apostle as a 'witness to the resurrection' (Acts 1:22). Like Mary, we must somehow hear our name pronounced, must hear ourselves being addressed and regarded by Love, before we can recognize this Christ in our midst. And like Mary, we usually need to start with the concrete encounter before we move to the universal experience available to all." (page 192)

In pairs, take two minutes each to talk about the aspects of this Mary Magdalene quotation that resonate with you and your life experience. With what do you connect? By what are you repelled?

When it's your turn to listen, do not ask questions, interrupt, or interject in any way. Allow for silence and simply thank your partner for sharing. This paired exercise is simply to listen to each other.

**Group Sharing (with Talking Stick):**
The group takes two minutes to sit with and digest the following quotations. Notice what draws you; notice anything you resist.

> "I would insist that the foundation of Jesus's social program is what I will call *non-idolatry*, or *the withdrawing of your enthrallment from all kingdoms except the Kingdom of God*. . . . Nonattachment (freedom from full or final loyalties to man-made domination systems) is the best way I know of protecting people from religious zealotry or any kind of antagonistic thinking or behavior. *There is nothing to be against, but just keep concentrating on the Big Thing you are for!* (Think Francis of Assisi and Mother Teresa.)" (page 197)

> "Paul's notion of sin comes amazingly close to our present understanding of addiction. . . . *The addict, or sinner, does not actually enjoy the world as much as he or she is enslaved to it,* in Paul's understanding. Jesus had come to offer us a true alternative social order here and not just a 'way to heaven' later." (pages 197–198)

One person picks up the talking stick and begins sharing. As you listen to others, notice what thoughts and emotions arise within you. As you do this, do not debate, defend, or disagree with others, while they speak or when it is your turn to speak. (Fifteen minutes total are allocated for this round of group sharing.)

Facilitator closes the group with the bell and invites people to leave in silence.

**Solo Reflection at Home (Optional):**

**Exercise 1**

> "Very important, and an utterly new idea from Paul was that the

> Gospel was not about following some criteria *outside* of the human person—which he calls 'the law,' but that the locus of authority had changed to *inside* the human person." (page 199)

How have you experienced this locus of authority transition from *outside* to *inside* the human person in your own spirituality?

How has this affected your experience of the "good news" of the Gospel?

## Exercise 2

> "[Paul] would have agreed with Jesus, I think, that humans are punished *by* their sins more than *for* their sins." (page 196)

This week, read and re-read this quotation, and journal about the various layers of meaning that this has for you. You may want to reflect on:

> Different teachings you have heard about the nature of sin in the past.

> Your experiences of being punished *by* your sins rather than *for* them.

## Exercise 3

If you continue to practice a contemplative sit on your own this week, read this same line aloud as a lead-in/introduction to your practice:

> "[Paul] would have agreed with Jesus, I think, that humans are punished *by* their sins more than *for* their sins."

*Please read chapters 16, 17, and the Afterword before our next meeting.*

## WEEK VII OF VIII
## Chapters: 16, 17, and Afterword

**FACILITATOR:**

*Welcomes* the group and invites everyone to a minute of silence by way of settling in. Then the facilitator reads the following quotation:

> "If we've been kept from appreciating a cosmic notion of Christ up to now, it has not been because of bad will, ignorance, or obstinacy. It's because we have tried to understand a largely nondual notion with the dualistic mind that dominates Western rationalism and scientism. That will never work. Most of us were not told that we needed to install 'software' different from the either-or, problem-solving, all-or-nothing mind that we use to get us through the day. Only early Christianity, and many mystics along the way, tended to understand that contemplation is actually a different way of processing our experience—a radically different way of seeing—which most of us have to be taught." (page 203)

The group reflects on this in silence for another minute before moving into the solo reflection.

**Solo Reflection:**
Spend four minutes pondering the quotation and questions in your journal.

> "We became a formal and efficient religion that felt that its job was to tell people *what to see instead of how to see*." (page 211)

In what ways have you been told *"what to see instead of how to see"*?

How has this affected you?

In what ways have you told others *"what to see instead of how to see"*?

How has this affected you and your relationship with others?

**Pair Sharing:**
Spend one minute silently pondering the quotations and questions.

> "Authentic Christianity is not so much a belief system as a life-and-death system that shows you how to give away your life, how to give away your love, and eventually how to give away your death. Basically, how to *give away*—and in doing so, to connect with the world, with all other creatures, and with God." (pages 212–213)

> *"God comes to you disguised as your life."* (page 212)

How have you experienced this "giving away" of your life?

What are you being asked to give away right now as "God [is coming] to you disguised as your life"? What is that experience like?

Take two minutes each to speak. When it's your turn to listen, do not ask questions or speak in any way—even if you think you have something important to say. Give your partner time and space and allow for silence. Thank your partner for sharing.

*Lectio*

**FACILITATOR:**

***Reads*** the text for the *Lectio* slowly and clearly for the whole group to hear. Group members may read along with the text or choose to close their eyes and simply listen. (This first reading is to help the group familiarize themselves with the quotation.)

"If Christ represents the resurrected state, then Jesus represents the crucified/resurrecting path of getting there. If Christ is the source and goal, then Jesus is the path from that source toward the goal of divine unity with all things." (page 216) (Pause)

**Reads** the passage slowly and clearly a second time, inviting the group to allow the quotation to "wash over them," noticing which word or phrase stands out for them.

After a minute of silence, one person picks up the talking stick and briefly shares the word or phrase that stood out for them. Then, going around in a circle, everyone takes a turn to briefly share the word or phrase that stood out for them. If anyone chooses not to share a word or phrase, they simply say "pass" and hand the talking stick to the next person. (Two minutes total are allocated for this round of group sharing.)

### Solo Reflection:
Take a minute in silence to linger over a word or phrase; "to focus on it until it engages your body, your heart, your awareness of the physical [and unseen] world around you." (page 8)

### FACILITATOR:

**Invites** each person in the group to take the talking stick and share, in just a few sentences, the connection between the word or phrase and their life. (Twelve minutes total are allocated for this round of group sharing.)

**Reads** the passage one last time and the group sits in contemplative silence for three minutes, allowing the divine lesson to sink in and settle within their whole being.

**Solo Reflection:**
Take five minutes to read over this poem more than once and respond to the questions in your journal.

### LOVE AFTER LOVE

*The time will come*
*when, with elation,*
*you will greet yourself arriving*
*at your own door, in your own mirror,*
*and each will smile at the other's welcome,*

*and say, sit here. Eat.*
*You will love again the stranger who was yourself.*
*Give wine. Give bread. Give back your heart*
*to itself, to the stranger who has loved you*

*all your life, whom you ignored*
*for another, who knows you by heart.*
*Take down the love letters from the bookshelf,*

*the photographs, the desperate notes,*
*peel your own image from the mirror.*
*Sit. Feast on your life.*

—Derek Walcott (page 234)

What emotions does it evoke within you?

What line or lines strike you the most?

Describe the *"stranger who has loved you . . . who knows you by heart."*
(Even with just a word or two—the first words that come to you.)

**Pair Sharing:**
One partner slowly reads Practice I on page 224 to the other (allow five minutes for each reading).

Once you have finished reading, give your partner a minute to return their full presence to the room.

Invite your partner, if they wish, to jot down any notes or reflections they might have in their journal.

Once they are finished writing, switch roles and repeat the process.

**Group Sharing (with Talking Stick):**

**FACILITATOR:**

*Invites* the group to get comfortable in their seats, to ground themselves in their bodies, and to take a few quiet, deep breaths as they wait for the reading to begin.

*Reads* aloud "The Divine Mirror" from pages 226–229.

*Gives* the group an opportunity to engage for five minutes total in a *brief* round of sharing, using the following question:

"What is resonating with you in this moment?" (The facilitator may want to repeat this question as the talking stick is passed around.)

*Closes* the group with the bell and invites people to leave in silence.

## Solo Reflection at Home (Optional):

## Exercise 1

Choosing either Practice I (beginning on page 224) or Practice II (beginning on page 225), take some solo time to repeat this practice during the week.

What is evoked within you now as you return to this practice on your own?

How is this different from your experience of practicing with a partner or the group?

What is the benefit of having other people in your life that can participate in spiritual practices with you?

## Exercise 2

Read through the poem "Love After Love" (page 234) a few times and notice which words, phrases, or images stand out to you now.

What emotions are you aware of as you reflect?

What does *"Take down the love letters from the bookshelf"* mean to you in this reading?

If God were to tell you to *"peel your own image from the mirror. Sit. Feast on your life"* today, what would that mean to you?

## Exercise 3

"In our Living School here in New Mexico we teach a methodology that we call our 'tricycle.' It moves forward on three wheels:

*Experience, Scripture, and Tradition,* which must be allowed to regulate and balance one another. Very few Christians were given permission, or training, in riding all three wheels together, much less allowing experience to be the front wheel. We also *try to ride all three wheels in a 'rational' way,* knowing that if we give reason its own wheel, it will end up driving the whole car." (page 213)

What has been your experience of this "tricycle" of *"Experience, Scripture, and Tradition"* during the formative years of your faith/spiritual practice?

What is your experience of this "tricycle" now? What is influencing that experience?

**Exercise 4**

"You discover a Larger Self underneath. You decide not to push yourself to the front of the line, and something much better happens in the back of the line. You let go of your narcissistic anger, and you find that you start feeling much happier. You surrender your need to control your partner, and finally the relationship blossoms. Yet each time it is a choice—and each time it is a kind of dying." (pages 218–219)

Using this quotation as a lead-in, practice a contemplative sit of your own at some point during the week. Take a few moments to read the passage first, then settle yourself into your seat and slowly read the same quotation out loud. You may wish to set a timer or a prayer bell so that you know when to finish.

*Please read the Appendixes before our next meeting.*

## WEEK VIII OF VIII
Appendixes

**FACILITATOR:**

*Invites* the group to begin with a contemplative sit for ten minutes, after reading the following quotation from Appendix II:

> "There is a crack in everything, that's how the light gets in."
> —Leonard Cohen (page 244)

## Solo Reflection:
Reflect on the following summaries of each of The Four Worldviews (as outlined in Appendix I) and then respond to the questions below in your journal (fifteen minutes are allocated for this reflection):

> The *material worldview* believes "that the outer, visible universe is the ultimate and 'real' world. People of this worldview have given us science, engineering, medicine, and much of what we now call 'civilization.'. . . A material worldview tends to create highly consumer-oriented and competitive cultures, which are often preoccupied with scarcity, since material goods are always limited." (page 238)

> "The *spiritual worldview* characterizes many forms of religion and some idealistic philosophies that recognize the primacy and finality of spirit, consciousness, the invisible world behind all manifestations. . . . But taken too far it can become ethereal and disembodied, disregarding ordinary human needs and denying the need for good psychology, anthropology, or societal issues of peace and justice. The spiritual worldview, taken too seriously, has little concern for the earth, the neighbor, or justice, because it considers this world largely as an illusion." (page 238)

"Those holding . . . the *priestly worldview* are generally sophisticated, trained, and experienced people and traditions that feel their job is to help us put matter and Spirit together. They are the holders of the law, the scriptures, and the rituals; they include gurus, ministers, therapists, and sacred communities. People of the priestly worldview help us make good connections that are not always obvious between the material and spiritual worlds. . . . [T]his view assumes that the two worlds are actually separate and need someone to bind them back together. . . . It describes what most of us think of as organized religion and much of the self-help world." (pages 238–239)

"The *incarnational worldview*, [is one] in which matter and Spirit are understood to have never been separate. Matter and spirit reveal and manifest each other. *This view relies more on awakening than joining, more on seeing than obeying, more on growth in consciousness and love than on clergy, experts, morality, scriptures, or rituals. The code word I am using in this entire book for this worldview is simply 'Christ.'* . . . In Christian history, we see the *incarnational worldview* most strongly in the early Eastern Fathers, Celtic spirituality, many mystics who combined prayer with intense social involvement, Franciscanism in general, many nature mystics, and contemporary eco-spirituality." (page 239)

What resonates with you from each of the worldviews?

What do you resist from each of the worldviews?

How does your experience of reading this book and/or participating in this group relate to each of these worldviews?

What changes have taken place within you as a result of your participation?

## Pair Sharing:

> *"The incarnational worldview grounds Christian holiness in objective and ontological reality instead of just moral behavior. . . . If it is truly incarnational Christianity, then it is always 'hands-on' religion and not solely esotericism, belief systems, or priestly mediation."* (page 240)

With a partner, take five minutes each to share your answers to the above questions (from the Solo Reflection section). As you listen, pay particular attention to your quality of listening and how you are present to your partner, regardless of your own opinions and experiences. As you notice your own opinions or experiences arising, release their grip on your attention and refocus on what your partner is sharing.

## Group Sharing (with Talking Stick):

Take three minutes of quiet to individually reflect on aspects of the Pattern of Spiritual Transformation: Order, Disorder, Reorder (a summary is below, but you may wish to review the longer outline on pages 244–246):

**Order**: "invariably operates from a worldview of scarcity and hardly ever from abundance."

**Disorder**: "the 'fall' . . . is *necessary in some form* if any real growth is to occur; but some of us find this stage so uncomfortable we try to flee back to our first created order—even if it is killing us."

**Reorder**: "It is an insistence on going *through—not under, over, or around*. . . . These wise ones have stopped overreacting but also overdefending. They are usually a minority of humans."

Which of these three—Order, Disorder, or Reorder—best describes your current experience and how is that impacting how you feel right now? Using the talking stick, take turns to share your reflections on any aspect of these questions with the group. (Twenty minutes total are allocated for this final round of group sharing.)

Don't plan what you will say. When it is your turn, the facilitator will read the question again to allow you to speak from the heart, sharing whatever is coming up for you at that very moment.

Listen carefully to others as they speak. Notice what distracts you, what makes you reactive, and practice coming back to attentive listening. Stay with your experience of listening to others, whether they speak of challenges and difficulties or encouragements and hopes.

Facilitator closes the group with the bell and invites people to leave in silence.

*Thank you very much for taking part in this group practice guide. We encourage you to look back over your notes, to journal, to reflect, and, most importantly, to continue with the spiritual practices that have resonated with you over these eight sessions.*

# EMBODIMENT

## Group Guide

Welcome to the Embodiment practice group for *The Universal Christ: How a Forgotten Reality Can Change Everything We See, Hope For, and Believe*, Fr. Richard Rohr's most important book to date. This Group Guide provides instructions for each practice group session. There will also be a facilitator for your group, who will explain the practices, keep time, guide group sharing, and answer questions you may have about the group process and practices.

Before the first gathering, please read and commit to the following.

**Agreements for Group Participation**

- Reading the book.
- Respecting the group guidelines and the role of the facilitator.
- No commenting or interrupting when a group member is sharing.
- Holding confidentiality throughout the course of the group sessions, inside and outside of the sessions.
- Sharing *only* one's own personal story.

**Modalities for Participation**

The Group Guide has been formulated in a way that allows for a balance of group work, pair sharing, and solo reflection:

- **Group Work** involves group sharing in a circle using a "talking stick" (introduced by the facilitator at the first session), reflective *Lectio* practice, and contemplative sit. It is a time to deepen into a felt sense of the mind and body of Christ.
- **Pair Sharing** will give individuals an opportunity to share what is true for them with one other person and to practice being an attentive listening presence to their partners.

- **Solo Reflection** is time for individuals to process the content as it relates to their own lives.

## Group Sharing Guidelines

- Gather in a circle.
- Use the talking stick.
- Speak in the moment (try not to prepare something in advance).
- Speak from the heart (speak what is *true* for you, regardless of whether it is "right").
- Be lean of speech (share a few sentences at most, with time to pause and ponder in between).
- Listen from the heart (respect the honest sharing of others and listen in a way that moves you beyond thinking of what this means to *you*; instead, what does this mean to the person who is sharing?).
- Respect confidentiality in this sacred space (what is shared in the group *must* stay in the group; otherwise the group cannot grow together).

In group sharing, be mindful of not speaking or commenting when individuals are sharing. Practicing presence, by not speaking too much and listening in silence, is an important part of group sessions. Each week, bring your copy of *The Universal Christ*, this Group Guide, a journal for recording your reflections, and a Bible to the session.

*Before the first session, read chapters 1 and 2 of The Universal Christ.*

# EMBODIMENT

**WEEK I OF VIII**
**Chapters: 1 and 2**

**FACILITATOR:**

*Invites* the group to get comfortable, take some deep breaths, let go of the stresses of the day, and sit in silence for one minute.

**Solo Reflection:**
Spend one minute pondering this quotation and question in your journal.

> "But God loves things by becoming them.
> God loves things by uniting with them, not by excluding them." (page 16)

What impact does this have on you, in this very moment?

**Pair Sharing:**
Spend one minute pondering this quotation.

> "John's choice of an active verb ('*The true light . . . was coming into the world*,' 1:9), shows us that the Christ Mystery is not a one-time event, but an ongoing process throughout time—as constant as the light that fills the universe. And 'God saw that light was good' (Genesis 1:3). Hold on to that!" (page 14)

Reflect on this "ongoing process throughout time." Can you identify an experience of the light of the Christ Mystery in your own life? Take turns sharing in pairs for three minutes each. When it's your turn to listen, do not ask questions, interrupt, or interject in any way. Allow for silence and simply thank your partner for sharing. This paired exercise is simply to become more present through listening to each other.

*Lectio*

**FACILITATOR:**

***Reads*** the text below slowly and clearly for the whole group to hear. Group members may read along with the text or choose to close their eyes and simply listen. (This first reading is to help the group familiarize themselves with the quotation.)

> *"Christ is everywhere.*
> *In Him every kind of life has a meaning and a solid connection."* (page 8)

***Reads*** the passage slowly and clearly a second time. Each person allows the quotation to "wash over them," noticing which word or phrase stands out for them.

### Group Sharing (with Talking Stick):

After a few moments of silence, one person picks up the talking stick and briefly shares the word or phrase that stood out for them. Then, going around in a circle, everyone takes a turn to briefly share the word or phrase that stood out for them. If anyone chooses not to share a word or phrase, they simply say "pass'" and hand the talking stick to the next person. (Two minutes total are allocated for this round of group sharing.)

### Solo Reflection:

In silence, take one minute to linger over this word or phrase; "to focus on it until it engages your body, your heart, your awareness of the physical [and unseen] world around you." (page 8)

**FACILITATOR:**

***Invites*** each person to take the talking stick and share, in just a few sentences, the connection between the word or phrase and their life.

(Fifteen minutes total are allocated for this round of group sharing.)

*Reads* the passage one last time. The group sits in contemplative silence for two minutes, allowing the *Lectio* to sink in and settle within their whole being.

## Solo Reflection:

Take two minutes to read this quotation and reflect on the questions in your journal.

> "An *incarnational worldview* is the profound recognition of the presence of the divine in literally "every thing" and "every one." It is the key to mental and spiritual health, as well as to a kind of basic contentment and happiness." (page 18)

In your own life, how are you seeing the divine in "every thing"?

How is this affecting your spiritual health, your basic contentment and happiness?

## Pair Sharing:

Spend two minutes pondering these quotations.

> "As long as we keep God imprisoned in a retributive frame instead of a restorative frame, we really have no substantial good news; it is neither good nor new, but the same old tired story line of history. We pull God down to our level." (pages 28–29)

> "Building on 2 Peter 1:4, where the author says, 'He has given us something very great and wonderful . . . you are *able to share the divine nature!*' This is Christianity's core good news and only transformative message." (pages 27–28)

In pairs, share for two minutes each on the contrasts you noticed between the quotations above.

**Group Sharing (with Talking Stick):**
Take one minute to reflect on this passage:

> "The sacramental principle is this: *Begin with a concrete moment of encounter, based in this physical world, and the soul universalizes from there, so that what is true here becomes true everywhere else too.* And so the spiritual journey proceeds with ever-greater circles of inclusion into the One Holy Mystery! But it always starts with what many wisely call the 'scandal of the particular.'" (page 31)

Your facilitator will remind you of the talking stick guidelines. Use the talking stick to share your thoughts on "the spiritual journey proceeds with ever-great circles of inclusion." (Ten minutes total are allocated for this round of group sharing.)

**FACILITATOR:**

*Invites* the group to end the session by practicing a contemplative sit based on the Ignatian *Daily Examen*—a prayerful reflection on the events of the day in order to discern God's presence and guidance in our lives.

*Invites* group members to take a moment to notice their posture; become comfortable in their seat; sit slightly forward, until their spine is no longer touching the back of the seat. (Pause)

Become aware of both feet touching the floor, grounding you in the present moment. (Pause) Focus on your back and neck. Find your most neutral position, taking a moment to allow your back and neck to align. (Pause) Lower your gaze and focus on a point on the floor in front of you. Or, close your eyes if that is more comfortable. (Pause)

Cast your mind back over this time together. (Pause) Notice those experiences that were rich. (Pause) Those moments that gave you a sense of energy. (Pause) Where you felt connected to other people and the world around you. (Pause) Moments where you felt at one with yourself. (Pause)

Notice your breathing. Don't change it; just become aware of it. (Pause) Notice how your body feels as you reflect on this day. (Pause)

Now notice those experiences you've had that were not so rich. (Pause) Moments that diminished your sense of energy. (Pause) Where you felt disconnected from other people and the world around you. (Pause)

Notice your breathing and your body once more. (Pause) How does your body feel as you reflect on the moments where you did not feel fully connected today? (Pause)

Finally, notice whether you felt a sense of Holy Mystery during our time. It might have been during moments of connection and love. (Pause) It might have been during moments of disconnection and suffering. (Pause) Or you may not have sensed the Holy Mystery at all. That's ok. (Pause)

Now simply rest in silence, allowing yourself to reflect, meditate, or simply to breathe—whichever feels most appropriate right now.

*Rings* the prayer bell after ten minutes to indicate that the contemplative sit has finished, and the session has ended.

**Solo Reflection at Home (Optional):**

**Exercise 1**

Remember a time in your life when you were confused by something you were learning or when your life seemed a little out of control. What was happening? What effect did it have on you? (Your reflections will not be shared with the group.)

Is there something in that experience that you might see differently or more deeply after reading this book?

*Please read chapters 3 and 4 before our next meeting.*

## WEEK II OF VIII
## Chapters: 3 and 4

**FACILITATOR:**

*Reads* the following quotation:

> "*I have never been separate from God, nor can I be, except in my mind.*" (page 45)

*Invites* the group to get comfortable, take some deep breaths, let go of the stresses of the day, and sit in silence for one minute. (The facilitator may choose to use a prayer bell to mark the opening and closing of this short, one-minute sit.)

*Reads* the quotation again, waits for another minute, then invites participants into solo reflection.

## Solo Reflection:
Spend two minutes pondering the quotations and question in your journal.

> "'There is only Christ. He is everything and he is in everything' (Colossians 3:11)." (page 48)

> "Paul calls this bigger Divine identity the 'mystery of his purpose, the hidden plan he so kindly made *en Cristo* from the very beginning' (Ephesians 1:9). Today, we might call it the 'collective unconscious.'" (page 44)

What comes up for you as you reflect on these?

**Pair Sharing:**
One partner slowly reads the following quotation out loud. Pause, then repeat it twice more to let the words sink in:

> *"I have never been separate from God, nor can I be, except in my mind."* (page 45)

Share your responses to the following for two minutes each. When it's your turn to listen, do not ask questions, interrupt, or interject in any way. Allow for silence and simply thank your partner for sharing. This paired exercise is simply to listen to each other.

As you listened to the above quotation, what arose for you:

On a cognitive level? (Thoughts)

On an emotional level? (Feelings)

On a physiological level? (Sensations)

**Group Sharing (with Talking Stick):**
Take one minute to silently reflect on this quotation:

> "I cannot help but think that future generations will label the first two thousand years of Christianity 'early Christianity.' They will, I believe, draw out more and more of the massive implications of this understanding of a Cosmic Christ." (page 48)

Your facilitator will review the Group Sharing Guidelines. Then you will take turns sharing your thoughts with the group. (Twenty minutes total are allocated for this round of group sharing.)

## Solo Reflection:
Take two minutes to read this quotation and reflect in your journal.

> *"The proof that you are a Christian is that you can see Christ everywhere else."* (page 51)

Reflect on how and where you see Christ in the world around you.

Take two minutes to read this quotation and focus in this way.

> *"Pause to focus on an incarnation of God's love apparent near you right now. You must risk it!"* (page 52)

## Pair Sharing:
Take two minutes in silent reflection on the following:

> *"Anything that draws you out of yourself in a positive way—for all practical purposes—is operating as God for you at that moment. How else can the journey begin? How else are you drawn forward, now not by idle beliefs but by inner aliveness? God needs something to seduce you out and beyond yourself, so God uses three things in particular: goodness, truth, and beauty."* (page 52)

Remember a time when the goodness of another person really inspired you.

Think of something you read, heard, or watched whose truth brought a *deep resonance* to your soul.

Remember a beautiful piece of art, music, or literature, or an experience in nature that filled you with wonder.

Choose one of these experiences that brought goodness, truth, and/or beauty alive for you. Share with your partner for two minutes each about how this experience has shaped your "inner aliveness" and your experience of God.

**Group Sharing (with Talking Stick):**
Take two minutes to reflect on these quotes in silence.

> "*I have never met a truly compassionate or loving human being who did not have a foundational and even deep trust in the inherent goodness of human nature.*" (page 63)

> "It is interesting that Jesus emphasized the absolute centrality of inner motivation and intention more than outer behavior, spending almost half of the Sermon on the Mount on this subject (see Matthew 5:20–6:18). We must—yes, *must*—make a daily and even hourly choice to focus on the good, the true, and the beautiful." (page 64)

Use the talking stick to share your thoughts with the group. (Fifteen minutes total are allocated for this round of group sharing.)

Facilitator closes the group with the bell and invites people to leave in silence.

**Solo Reflection at Home (Optional):**

### Exercise 1

> "Studies like the ones done by the neuroscientist Rick Hanson show that we must consciously hold on to a positive thought or feeling for a minimum of fifteen seconds before it leaves any imprint in the neurons. The whole dynamic, in fact, is called the Velcro/Teflon theory of the mind. We are more attracted to the problem than the solution, you might say." (page 64)

"The only way, then, to increase authentic spirituality is to *deliberately practice* actually enjoying a positive response and a grateful heart. And the benefits are very real. By following through on conscious choices, we can rewire our responses toward love, trust, and patience. Neuroscience calls this '*neuroplasticity*.'" (page 64)

For the next week, "*deliberately practice* actually enjoying a positive response and a grateful heart" for a minimum of fifteen seconds every day. Write down the thought and the emotion you experience after the thought, for each day of the week.

**Please read chapters 5, 6, and 7 before our next meeting.**

## WEEK III OF VIII
## Chapters: 5 through 7

**FACILITATOR:**

*Welcomes* the group and invites everyone to observe a minute of silence by way of settling into their seats and feeling present to themselves and the rest of the group.

## Solo Reflection:
Take two minutes to read this quotation and reflect on the question in your journal.

> "Remember, the only thing that separates you from God is *the thought* that you are separate from God!" (page 80)

What word or phrase strikes you? What does this evoke within you?

## Pair Sharing:

> "Similarly, as I look at the things and people I have tried to love in my life, I would have to say, 'They made me do it!' It was the inherent goodness, inner beauty, vulnerability, deep honesty, or generosity of spirit from the other side that drew me out of myself and toward them. In a very real sense, I did not initiate love toward them. Rather, it was taken from me! It was pulled out of me—by them." (page 77)

In pairs, reflect for two minutes each on this quote. Have you had similar or differing experiences of love in your life? What have these experiences been like for you? How do they affect you today?

**FACILITATOR:**

*Reads* the following quotations to the group:

> "Many educated and sophisticated people are not willing to submit to indirect, subversive, and intuitive knowing, which is probably why they rely far too much on external law and ritual behavior to achieve their spiritual purposes." (pages 85–86)

> "Many of us have been trained to write off these inner voices as mere emotion, religious conditioning, or psychological manipulation. Perhaps they sometimes are, but often they are *not*. . . . I personally was so trained *not* to trust those voices that I think I often did not hear the voice of God to me, or what Abraham Lincoln called the 'better angels of our nature.'" (pages 86, 89)

*Invites* the group to prepare for a contemplative sit and reads the same quotations again.

*Rings* a prayer bell to indicate that the contemplative sit has begun. After ten minutes, the facilitator rings a prayer bell to indicate that the contemplative sit has finished.

**Solo Reflection:**
Take five minutes to read this quotation and reflect on the questions in your journal.

> "How does anyone achieve such a holding together of opposites—things like inner acceptance and outer resistance, intense suffering and perfect freedom, my little self and an infinite God, sensuality and intense spirituality, the need to blame somebody and the freedom to blame nobody? . . . Christ [is] a universally available 'voice' that calls all things to *become whole and true to themselves*. God's two main tools in this direction, from every appearance, seem to be

great love and great suffering—and often great love that *invariably leads* to great suffering." (page 83)

Reflect on a time in your life when you experienced great love or great suffering. What happened? Who was involved?

What emotions did you feel at that time? Can you see the tension of opposites as you look back on the situation (e.g. "intense suffering and perfect freedom, my little self and an infinite God")?

Did this experience lead you to become more *"whole and true"* to yourself? If so, in what way(s)? If not, what effect did this experience have on you?

How does this experience continue to influence you today?

**Pair Sharing:**

> *"There is no such thing as a nonpolitical Christianity.* To refuse to critique the system of the status quo is to fully support it." (page 94)

In pairs, reflect for three minutes each on these questions.

How do you step back and see the systems at play, including privilege, nationhood, or religion? (page 94) (Share at least one specific example.)

How do you try and hold yourself above these systems or apart from them? (page 94)

*Lectio*

**FACILITATOR:**

**Reads** the following quotation slowly and clearly for the whole group to hear. Group members may read along with the text or choose to close their eyes and simply listen. (This first reading is to help the group familiarize themselves with the quotation.)

> "God *protects us into* and *through* death, just as the Father did with Jesus." (page 93)

**Reads** the passage slowly and clearly a second time. Each person allows the quotation to "wash over them," noticing which word or phrase stands out for them.

## Group Sharing (with Talking Stick):

After a few moments of silence, one person picks up the talking stick and briefly shares the word or phrase that stood out for them. Then, going around in a circle, everyone takes a turn to briefly share the word or phrase that stood out for them. If anyone chooses not to share a word or phrase, they simply say "pass'" and hand the talking stick to the next person. (Two minutes total are allocated for this round of group sharing.)

## Solo Reflection:

In silence, take one minute to linger over this word or phrase; "to focus on it until it engages your body, your heart, your awareness of the physical [and unseen] world around you." (page 8)

**FACILITATOR:**

**Invites** each person to take the talking stick and share, in just a few sentences, the connection between the word or phrase and their life. (Fifteen minutes total are allocated for this round of group sharing.)

***Reads*** the passage one last time. The group sits in contemplative silence, allowing the *Lectio* to sink in and settle within their whole being.

***Rings*** the prayer bell after five minutes to indicate that the contemplative sit has finished, and the session has ended.

**Solo Reflection at Home (Optional):**

**Exercise 1**

Leading in with the following quotation, practice another contemplative sit of your own this week. You may wish to set a timer or a prayer bell so that you know when to finish.

> "This point is worth sitting with for a few moments.
> *Every time you take in a breath, you are repeating the pattern of taking spirit into matter, and thus repeating the first creation of Adam.*
> *And every time you breathe out, you are repeating the pattern of returning spirit to the material universe.* In a way, every exhalation is a 'little dying' as we pay the price of inspiriting the world. Your simple breathing models your entire vocation as a human being. You are an incarnation, like Christ, of matter and spirit operating as one." (page 99)

If you wish, write down a reflection on your experience of this sit.

**Exercise 2**

> "As C. G. Jung inscribed over his doorway, *Vocatus atque non vocatus, Deus aderit*, 'Invoked or not invoked, God is still present.'" (page 100)

Write in your journal a few experiences and situations in your week where God was "invoked."

What are these experiences like for you?

Write down an experience in your week where God was "not invoked," but your faith attested to God being present.

What is this experience like for you?

Is there any difference between the two types of experiences? Why or why not?

**Exercise 3**

> *"God has worked anonymously since the very beginning—it has always been an inside and secret sort of job. The Spirit seems to work best underground. When aboveground, humans start fighting about it."* (page 100)

Notice (and note in your journal) where and when you want to contribute "aboveground," in a visible way, this week.

Notice where and when you want to contribute anonymously, "underground," in a secret way, this week.

Energetically, what difference did these differing orientations make on how you contributed to others?

*Please read chapters 8, 9, and 10 before our next meeting.*

# WEEK IV OF VIII
## Chapters: 8 through 10

**FACILITATOR:**

*Welcomes* the group and invites everyone to begin with a contemplative sit.

*Slowly reads* the quotation and then gives the group three minutes to sit in silence:

> "There must be a way to be both *here* and in the *depth of here.* Jesus is the here, Christ is the depth of here." (page 118)

## Solo Reflection:
Take five minutes to reflect on the quotations and questions in your journal.

> "The Apostles' Creed does not once mention love, service, hope, the 'least of the brothers and sisters,' or even forgiveness—anything, actually, that is remotely *actionable*. It's a vision and philosophy statement with no mission statement, as it were. Twice we are reminded that God is almighty, yet nowhere do we hear mention that God is also *all suffering* or *all vulnerable*." (page 104)

In what ways has your experience of Christian spirituality been more a "philosophy statement with no mission statement"?

To what degree have you experienced God as being all suffering or all vulnerable, as well as almighty?

> "Humanity now needs a Jesus who is historical, relevant for real life, physical and concrete, like we are. A Jesus whose life can save you even more than his death. A Jesus we can practically imitate, and

who sets the bar for what it means to be fully human. And a Christ who is big enough to hold all creation together in one harmonious unity." (page 107)

Write down any thoughts or hopes that arise within you in response to this second quotation.

**Pair Sharing:**
Take two minutes to silently read through the following quotations and notice what resonates with you.

> "As I watch Catholics receive communion at Mass, I notice that some, after taking the bread and wine, turn toward the altar or the sacred box that reserves the bread and bow or genuflect as a gesture of respect—as if the Presence were still over there.... Don't they realize that the Eucharist was supposed to be a full transference of identity to *them*? They themselves are now the living, moving tabernacle, just like the Ark of the Covenant. Is this too much for them to imagine? Does it seem presumptuous and impossible? It appears so." (page 109)

> "'I have known many Evangelicals who 'received Jesus into their hearts' but still felt the need to 'get saved' again every Friday night. Did they not believe that a real transformation happened if they made a genuine surrender and reconnected to their Source? Most of us understandably start the journey assuming that God is 'up there,' and our job is to transcend this world to find 'him.'" (page 110)

In pairs, share which aspect(s) of the quotations resonate with you. (Allow three minutes for each person.)

Then share your thoughts on one or both of these excerpts from the quotations, for two minutes each:

> "Don't they realize that the Eucharist was supposed to be a full transference of identity to *them*?"

> "Most of us understandably start the journey assuming that God is 'up there,' and our job is to transcend this world to find 'him.'"

**Group Sharing (with Talking Stick):**

**FACILITATOR:**

**Reminds** the group to use the talking stick to share their reflections with the group.

**Reads** the quotations below.

> "Remember, the archetypal encounter between doubting Thomas and the Risen Jesus (John 20:19–28) is not really a story about believing in the fact of the resurrection, but a story about believing that someone could *be wounded and also resurrected at the same time!*" (page 111)

> "'Put your finger here,' Jesus says to Thomas (20:27). And, like Thomas, we are indeed wounded and resurrected at the same time, all of us. In fact, this might be the primary pastoral message of the whole Gospel." (page 111)

Take one minute to reflect on these quotations and your own experience of being "wounded and resurrected at the same time." Each member is invited to share with the group, using the talking stick. (Fifteen minutes total are allocated for this round of group sharing.)

**Solo Reflection:**
Take two minutes to read this quotation and reflect on the questions in your journal.

> "We need to go into the depths of things—and to find God's spirit there. Whether they come through psychology, trained spiritual direction, the Enneagram, Myers-Briggs typology, grief and bereavement work, or other models such as Integral Theory or wilderness training, these tools help us to examine and to trust interiority and depth as never before." (page 115)

What tools, models, approaches, and experiences have been helpful for you to understand "the depths of things"?

What is something significant you have learned about yourself in this group?

**Pair Sharing:**
In pairs, share what comes up for you as you read and reflect on these quotations. (Allow three minutes for each person.)

> "The first incarnation (creation) is symbolized by Sophia-Incarnate, a beautiful, feminine, multicolored, graceful Mary.
>
> She is invariably offering us Jesus, God incarnated into vulnerability and nakedness.
>
> Mary became the Symbol of the First Universal Incarnation.
>
> She then hands the Second Incarnation to us, while remaining in the background; the focus is always on the child.
>
> Earth Mother presenting Spiritual Son, the two first stages of the Incarnation.
>
> Feminine Receptivity, handing on the fruit of her yes.
>
> And inviting us to offer our own yes.

There is a wholeness about this that many find very satisfying to the soul." (pages 123–124)

"We always had the feminine incarnation, in fact it was the first incarnation, and even better, it moved toward including all of us! *Mary is all of us* both *receiving and handing on the gift.*" (page 124)

## Lectio

**FACILITATOR:**

"*Mary is all of us* both *receiving and handing on the gift.*" (page 124)

**Reads** the text slowly and clearly for the whole group to hear. Group members may read along with the text or choose to close their eyes and simply listen. (This first reading is to help group members familiarize themselves with the quotation.)

**Reads** the text slowly and clearly a second time. Each person allows the quotation to "wash over them," noticing which word or phrase stands out for them.

After a few moments of silence, one person picks up the talking stick and briefly shares the word or phrase that stood out for them. Then, passing the talking stick around the circle, everyone takes a turn to briefly share the word or phrase that stood out for them. If anyone chooses not to share a word or phrase, they simply say "pass" and hand the talking stick to the next person. (Two minutes are allocated for this round of group sharing.)

### Solo Reflection:
In silence, take one minute to linger over this word or phrase; "to focus on it until it engages your body, your heart, your awareness of the physical [and unseen] world around you." (page 8)

FACILITATOR:

*Invites* each person to take the talking stick and share, in just a few sentences, the connection between the word or phrase and their life. (Fifteen minutes are allocated for this round of group sharing.)

*Reads* the passage one last time and invites the group to sit in contemplative silence for two minutes, allowing the divine lesson to sink in and settle within their whole being.

*Closes* the group with the bell and invites people to leave in silence.

## Solo Reflection at Home (Optional):

### Exercise 1

> "In Mary, humanity has said *our* eternal yes to God. A yes that cannot be undone. A corporate yes that overrides our many noes." (page 128)

Notice and write down the times and situations in your week where you are answering God or life with a no (for some, this might even include a no to relating your home reflection to Mary).

Notice and write down the times and situations in your week where you are answering God or life with a yes.

Where in your life *would* you like to answer God with a yes? Meditate on this (or even pray for this) in whatever way seems most fitting to you.

*Please read chapters 11 and 12 before our next meeting.*

# WEEK V OF VIII
## Chapters: 11 and 12

**FACILITATOR:**

*Reads* the following quotation:

> "Life is the destiny you are bound to refuse until you have consented to die."
> —W. H. Auden, "For the Time Being" (page 129)

*Invites* the group to get comfortable, take some deep breaths, let go of the stresses of the day, and sit in silence for one minute. (The facilitator may choose to use a prayer bell to mark the opening and closing of this short, one-minute sit.)

*Reads* the quotation again, waits for another minute, then invites participants into solo reflection.

## Solo Reflection:
Spend three minutes pondering the quotation and questions in your journal.

> "'Real Presence' . . . sets the stage for recipients to experience what I like to call 'carnal knowledge' of God, who is normally assumed to be Spirit. It seems that mere mind-knowing is not enough, because it does not engage the heart or soul. . . . But your only real prerequisite for participation or 'worthiness' is in fact *your capacity for presence* yourself." (page 131)

Take a moment to gently close your eyes and be a witness to all that is arising in you right now (thoughts, feelings, and bodily sensations). While staying connected to that inner world, gently open your eyes and note what you are observing.

In what ways have you assumed that God is merely Spirit?

> "Your only real prerequisite for participation... is in fact *your capacity for presence* yourself." God is as present to you as you are physically present to yourself.

Write down your gut reaction to this, even if it is an open question.

## Pair Sharing:

In pairs, take two minutes each to share any aspect of your solo reflection above or what comes up for you as you read and reflect on the quotation below.

> "The bread and the wine together are stand-ins for *the very elements of the universe*, which also enjoy and communicate the incarnate presence. Why did we resist this message so much?" (page 134)

## Group Sharing (with Talking Stick):

> "Love cannot be bought by some 'necessary sacrifice'; if it could, it would not and could not work its transformative effects. Try loving your spouse or children that way, and see where it gets you." (page 144)

> "John Duns Scotus (1266–1308), refused to see the Incarnation, and its final denouement on the cross, as a mere reaction to sin. Instead, [he and the Franciscans] claimed that the cross was a *freely chosen revelation of Total Love* on God's part." (page 143)

Take two minutes to reflect on these quotes in silence. Then use the talking stick to share your thoughts with the group. (Fifteen minutes total are allocated for this round of group sharing.)

As you listen to others, notice what thoughts and emotions arise within you.

As you speak, notice any inclination to defend or attack. The group is here to learn about your authentic *personal experience*—what is coming up for you in these moments as you hold the talking stick.

**Solo Reflection:**
Spend two minutes pondering this quotation and questions in your journal.

> "Most of us are still programmed to read the Scriptures according to the common laws of jurisprudence, which are hardly ever based on *restorative justice*.... Restorative justice was the amazing discovery of the Jewish prophets, in which Yahweh punished Israel by loving them even more! (Ezekiel 16:53ff)." (page 146)

What has been your experience of restorative justice?

When have you loved others more, in spite of their challenging behavior?

**Pair Sharing:**

> "A transformative religion must touch us at this primitive, brainstem level, or it is not transformative at all. History is continually graced with people who somehow learned to act beyond and outside their self-interest and for the good of the world, people who clearly operated by a power larger than their own.... I can't say how one becomes such a person. All I can presume is that they all had their Christ moments, in which they stopped denying their own shadows, stopped projecting those shadows elsewhere, and agreed to own their deepest identity in solidarity with the world." (page 152)

Take one minute to read through this quotation on your own. Then share, for two minutes each, about some or all of the following:

- Your own Christ moment
- Your own shadow
- Your sense of solidarity with the world at this point in time

**Group Sharing (with Talking Stick):**

*Lectio*

**FACILITATOR:**

***Reads*** the text for the *Lectio* slowly and clearly for the whole group to hear. Group members may read along with the text or choose to close their eyes and simply listen. (This first reading is to help the group familiarize themselves with the quotation.)

> "He did not come to change God's mind about us. It did not need changing. Jesus came to change our minds about God—and about ourselves—and about where goodness and evil really lie." (page 151)

***Reads*** the passage slowly and clearly a second time, inviting the group to allow the quotation to "wash over them," noticing which word or phrase stands out for them.

After a minute of silence, one person picks up the talking stick and briefly shares the word or phrase that stood out for them. Then, going around in a circle, everyone takes a turn to briefly share the word or phrase that stood out for them. If anyone chooses not to share a word or phrase, they simply say "pass" and hand the talking stick to the next person. (Two minutes total are allocated for this round of group sharing.)

**Solo Reflection:**
Take a minute in silence to linger over a word or phrase; "to focus on it until it engages your body, your heart, your awareness of the physical [and unseen] world around you." (page 8)

**FACILITATOR:**

*Invites* each person in the group to take the talking stick and share, in just a few sentences, the connection between the word or phrase and their life. (Fifteen minutes total are allocated for this round of group sharing.)

*Reads* the passage one last time and the group sits in contemplative silence for three minutes, allowing the divine lesson to sink in and settle within their whole being.

*Closes* the group with the bell and invites people to leave in silence.

**Solo Reflection at Home (Optional):**

**Exercise 1**

> "A Dialogue with the Crucified God"
>
> "Wait until you have an open, quiet, and solitary slot of time, then pray it out loud so your ears can hear your own words from your own mouth. In addition, I suggest that you place yourself before a tender image of the crucified Jesus that will allow you to both give and receive." (page 155)

Following the instructions above, read through "A Dialogue with the Crucified God" (pages 155–158) at some point this week. Journal anything that arises for you.

Please read chapters 13, 14, and 15 before our next meeting.

# WEEK VI OF VIII
## Chapters: 13 through 15

**FACILITATOR:**

*Welcomes* the group and invites everyone to a minute of silence by way of settling into their seats and feeling present to themselves and the rest of the group, then slowly reads the following quote, followed by one minute of silence:

> "Some mystics even go so far as to say that individual suffering doesn't exist at all—and that there is only one suffering, it is all the same, and it is all the suffering of God." (page 162)

## *Lectio*

**FACILITATOR:**

*Reads* the following text slowly and clearly for the whole group to hear. Group members may read along with the text or choose to close their eyes and simply listen. (This first reading is to help the group familiarize themselves with the quotation.)

> "A Crucified God is the dramatic symbol of *the one suffering* that God fully enters into *with us*—much more than just *for us*." (page 162)

*Reads* the passage slowly and clearly a second time. Each person allows the quotation to "wash over them," noticing which word or phrase stands out for them.

## Group Sharing (with Talking Stick):

After a few moments of silence, one person picks up the talking stick and briefly shares the word or phrase that stood out for them. Then, going around in a circle, everyone takes a turn to briefly share the word or phrase that stood out for them. If anyone chooses not to share a word or phrase, they simply say "pass'" and hand the talking stick to the next person. (Two minutes total are allocated for this round of group sharing.)

**Solo Reflection:**
In silence, take one minute to reflect on this word or phrase; "to focus on it until it engages your body, your heart, your awareness of the physical [and unseen] world around you." (page 8)

**FACILITATOR:**

*Invites* each person to take the talking stick and share, in just a few sentences, the connection between the word or phrase and their life. (Ten minutes total are allocated for this round of group sharing.)

*Reads* the passage one last time. The group sits in contemplative silence for two minutes, allowing the *Lectio* to sink in and settle within their whole being.

**Solo Reflection:**
Take three minutes to reflect on the quotation that your facilitator read to begin the session, as well as the quotation below, and respond to the following questions in your journal. (You will not be asked to share your responses.)

> "The only way out of deep sadness is to go *with it* and *through it*.... When I try to heroically do it alone, I slip into distractions, denials, and pretending—and *I do not learn suffering's softening lessons.*" (page 161)

What comes up for you when you hear the words "deep sadness"? What distractions, denials, or pretending do you use to avoid going "with it and through it"?

Is there someone in your life who could support you in approaching sadness differently?

**Pair Sharing:**
In pairs, take two minutes each to talk about the aspects of this quotation that resonate with you and your life experience:

> "Once I know that all suffering is both *our suffering and God's suffering*, I can better endure and trust the desolations and disappointments that come my way.... If I can recognize that all suffering and crucifixion (divine, planetary, human, animal) is 'one body' and will one day be transmuted into the 'one body' of cosmic resurrection (Philippians 3:21), I can at least live without going crazy or being permanently depressed." (page 167)

**Group Sharing (with Talking Stick):**
Take two minutes to silently reflect on these quotations and the following question:

> "As long as you operate inside any scarcity model, there will never be enough God or grace to go around. Jesus came to undo our notions of scarcity and tip us over into a worldview of absolute abundance—or what he would call the 'Kingdom of God.'" (pages 184–185)

> "The fragile ego always wants to set a boundary, a price, an entrance requirement of some sort. Many Christians sadly prefer ...a worldview of scarcity instead of the Gospel of divine abundance, and this constant resistance to Infinite Love is revealed in the biblical text itself." (page 173)

Reflect on your own worldview. Do you predominantly view your life from the perspective of scarcity or from the perspective of abundance?

**FACILITATOR:**

***Invites*** each person to take the talking stick and share, in a few sentences, their reflections with the group. As you listen to others, notice what thoughts and emotions arise within you. (Ten minutes total are allocated for this round of group sharing.)

**Solo Reflection:**

> "*It will really help you, Christian or not, if you can begin to see Jesus—and Christ—as coming out of Reality, naming it, giving it a face, not appearing to Reality from another world.* There is no group to join here, no need to sign on the dotted line, only a generous moment of recognition that the Inner and the Outer are one and the same.... If one's theology (view of God) does not significantly change one's anthropology (view of humanity), it is largely what we call a 'head trip.'" (page 174)

Take five minutes to slowly read over this quotation a few times and notice the words or phrases that stand out to you. Record these words in your journal and write a few lines about what they evoke within you.

Why might these words be striking a chord with you at this point in time?

**Pair Sharing:**
In pairs, take two minutes each to share what comes up for you as you read and reflect on this quotation. As you listen, practice the gift of fully accepting presence with your partner.

> "We usually have to let go of Jesus on one level before we can accept and believe in 'Jesus the Christ.' If your Jesus remains too small, too sentimental (e.g., 'Jesus, my personal boyfriend'), or too bound by time and culture, you do not get very far at all." (page 194)

**Group Sharing (with Talking Stick):**
Take one minute to sit with the following quotation, reflecting on how you have experienced this in your own life:

> "[Paul] would have agreed with Jesus, I think, that humans are punished *by* their sins more than *for* their sins." (page 196)

One person picks up the talking stick and begins sharing. As you listen to others, try not to prepare an answer, but trust your instinct for what to say when it is your turn to speak. (Ten minutes total are allocated for this round of group sharing.)

Facilitator closes the group with the bell and invites people to leave in silence.

**Solo Reflection at Home (Optional):**

**Exercise 1**

> "Very important, and an utterly new idea from Paul was that the Gospel was not about following some criteria *outside* of the human person—which he calls 'the law,' but that the locus of authority had changed to *inside* the human person." (page 199)

How have you experienced this transition from *outside* to *inside* the human person in your own spirituality?

How has this affected your experience of the "good news" of the Gospel?

**Exercise 2**

> "But remember, *the greater light you are, the greater shadow you cast*. And Paul is a huge light." (page 197)

As you discover more about yourself, your consciousness, and your spirituality, what kind of a shadow are you casting?

*Please read chapters 16, 17, and the Afterword before our next meeting.*

## WEEK VII OF VIII
Chapters: 16, 17, and Afterword

**FACILITATOR:**

*Welcomes* the group and invites everyone to a minute of silence by way of settling in. Then the facilitator reads the following quotation:

> "If we've been kept from appreciating a cosmic notion of Christ up to now, it has not been because of bad will, ignorance, or obstinacy. It's because we have tried to understand a largely nondual notion with the dualistic mind that dominates Western rationalism and scientism. That will never work. Most of us were not told that we needed to install 'software' different from the either-or, problem-solving, all-or-nothing mind that we use to get us through the day. Only early Christianity, and many mystics along the way, tended to understand that contemplation is actually a different way of processing our experience—a radically different way of seeing—which most of us have to be taught." (page 203)

The group reflects on this in silence for another minute before moving into the solo reflection.

## Solo Reflection:
Spend two minutes pondering the quotation and questions in your journal.

> "What many have begun to see is that you need to have a nondualistic, non-angry, and nonargumentative mind to process the *really big issues* with any depth or honesty, and most of us have not been effectively taught how to do that in practice. We were largely taught *what* to believe instead of *how* to believe." (page 207)

What is your experience of practicing this "nondualistic, non-angry, and nonargumentative" way of engaging in life?

In what ways has it impacted you, your relationships, and your quality of life?

**Pair Sharing:**
Spend two minutes silently pondering the quotation and questions in your journal.

> "In our Living School here in New Mexico we teach a methodology that we call our 'tricycle.' It moves forward on three wheels: *Experience, Scripture, and Tradition*, which must be allowed to regulate and balance one another. Very few Christians were given permission, or training, in riding all three wheels together, much less allowing experience to be the front wheel. We also *try to ride all three wheels in a 'rational' way,* knowing that if we give reason its own wheel, it will end up driving the whole car." (page 213)

What has been your experience of this "tricycle" of "*Experience, Scripture, and Tradition*" during the formative years of your faith/spiritual practice?

What is your experience of this "tricycle" now? What is influencing that experience?

Take two minutes each to share your reflections. As you listen, practice the gift of being a fully accepting presence with your partner. Resist any temptation to debate the merits or demerits of the "tricycle" ("if we give reason its own wheel, it will end up driving the whole car"). Instead, simply respond to the questions by sharing your experiences.

**FACILITATOR:**

*Invites* the group to practice a contemplative sit for fifteen minutes. The preparatory text for the sit is a quote from chapter 16:

> "You discover a Larger Self underneath. You decide not to push yourself to the front of the line, and something much better happens in the back of the line. You let go of your narcissistic anger, and you find that you start feeling much happier. You surrender your need to control your partner, and finally the relationship blossoms. Yet each time it is a choice—and each time it is a kind of dying." (pages 218–219)

**Solo Reflection:**
Take five minutes to read over this poem more than once and respond to the questions in your journal.

### LOVE AFTER LOVE

*The time will come
when, with elation,
you will greet yourself arriving
at your own door, in your own mirror,
and each will smile at the other's welcome,*

*and say, sit here. Eat.
You will love again the stranger who was yourself.
Give wine. Give bread. Give back your heart
to itself, to the stranger who has loved you*

*all your life, whom you ignored
for another, who knows you by heart.
Take down the love letters from the bookshelf,*

> *the photographs, the desperate notes,*
> *peel your own image from the mirror.*
> *Sit. Feast on your life.*

—Derek Walcott (page 234)

What is evoked from deep within you?

What line or lines strike you the most?

Describe the *"stranger who has loved you . . . who knows you by heart"* (even with just a word or two—the first words that come to you).

**Pair Sharing:**
One partner slowly reads Practice I on page 224 to the other (allow five minutes for each reading).

Once you have finished reading, give your partner a minute to return their full presence to the room.

Invite your partner, if they wish, to jot down any notes or reflections they might have.

Once they are finished writing, switch roles and repeat the process.

**Group Sharing (with Talking Stick):**

**FACILITATOR:**

*Invites* the group to get comfortable in their seats, to ground themselves in their bodies, and to take a few quiet, deep breaths as they wait for the reading to begin.

*Reads* aloud "The Divine Mirror" from pages 226–229.

***Gives*** the group an opportunity to engage for twelve minutes total in a round of sharing, using the following question:

"What is evoked from deep within you in this moment?" (The facilitator may want to repeat this question as the talking stick is passed around.)

***Closes*** the group with the bell and invites people to leave in silence.

**Solo Reflection at Home (Optional):**

**Exercise 1**

Choosing either Practice I (beginning on page 224) or Practice II (beginning on page 225), take some solo time to repeat this practice during the week.

What is evoked within you now as you return to this practice on your own?

How is this different from your experience of practicing with a partner or the group?

What is the benefit of having people in your life that can participate in spiritual practices with you?

**Exercise 2**

Read through the poem, "Love After Love" (page 234) a few times and notice which words, phrases, or images stand out for you now.

What emotions are you aware of as you reflect?

What does *"Take down the love letters from the bookshelf"* mean to you in this reading?

If God were to tell you to *"peel your own image from the mirror. Sit. Feast on your life"* today, what would that mean to you?

## Exercise 3

Reflect on the following quotations and respond to the questions in your journal:

> "Authentic Christianity is not so much a belief system as a life-and-death system that shows you how to give away your life, how to give away your love, and eventually how to give away your death. Basically, how to *give away*—and in doing so, to connect with the world, with all other creatures, and with God." (page 213)

> "God comes to you disguised as your life." (page 212)

How have you experienced this giving away of your life?

What are you being asked to give away right now? What is that experience like?

## Exercise 4

> "Spirituality is about honoring the human journey, loving it, and living it in all its wonder and tragedy. There is nothing really 'supernatural' about love and suffering. It is completely natural, taking us through the deep interplay of death and life, surrender and forgiveness, in all their basic and foundational manifestations. 'God comes to you disguised as your life.'" (page 212)

Using this quotation as a lead-in, practice a contemplative sit of your own at some point during the week. Take a few moments to read the passage first, then settle yourself into your seat and slowly read the same quotation out loud. You may wish to set a timer or a prayer bell so that you know when to finish.

*Please read the Appendixes before our next meeting.*

# WEEK VIII OF VIII
## Appendixes

**FACILITATOR:**

*Invites* the group to begin with a contemplative sit for four minutes, after reading the following quotation from Appendix II:

> "Conservatives must let go of their illusion that they can order and control the world through religion, money, war, or politics.... Liberals, however, must surrender their belief in permanent disorder, and their horror of all leadership, eldering, or authority, and find what was good, healthy, and deeply true about a foundational order. This will normally be experienced as a move toward humility and real community." (page 246)

## Solo Reflection:
Reflect on the following summaries of each of The Four Worldviews (as outlined in Appendix I) and then answer the questions in your journal (eight minutes are allocated for this reflection):

> The *material worldview* believes "that the outer, visible universe is the ultimate and 'real' world. People of this worldview have given us science, engineering, medicine, and much of what we now call 'civilization.'.... A material worldview tends to create highly consumer-oriented and competitive cultures, which are often preoccupied with scarcity, since material goods are always limited." (page 238)

> "The *spiritual worldview* characterizes many forms of religion and some idealistic philosophies that recognize the primacy and finality of spirit, consciousness, the invisible world behind all manifestations.... But taken too far it can become ethereal and disembodied, disregarding ordinary human needs and denying the need

for good psychology, anthropology, or societal issues of peace and justice. The spiritual worldview, taken too seriously, has little concern for the earth, the neighbor, or justice, because it considers this world largely as an illusion." (page 238)

"Those holding . . . the *priestly worldview* are generally sophisticated, trained, and experienced people and traditions that feel their job is to help us put matter and Spirit together. They are the holders of the law, the scriptures, and the rituals; they include gurus, ministers, therapists, and sacred communities. People of the priestly worldview help us make good connections that are not always obvious between the material and spiritual worlds. . . . this view assumes that the two worlds are actually separate and need someone to bind them back together. . . . It describes what most of us think of as organized religion and much of the self-help world." (pages 238–239)

"The *incarnational worldview,* [is one] in which matter and Spirit are understood to have never been separate. Matter and spirit reveal and manifest each other. *This view relies more on awakening than joining, more on seeing than obeying, more on growth in consciousness and love than on clergy, experts, morality, scriptures, or rituals. The code word I am using in this entire book for this worldview is simply 'Christ.'* . . . In Christian history, we see the *incarnational worldview* most strongly in the early Eastern Fathers, Celtic spirituality, many mystics who combined prayer with intense social involvement, Franciscanism in general, many nature mystics, and contemporary ecospirituality." (page 239)

What resonates with you from each of the worldviews?

What do you resist from each of the worldviews?

How does your experience of reading this book and/or participating in this group relate to each of these worldviews?

What changes have taken place within you as a result of your participation?

**Pair Sharing:**

> "We all come to wisdom at the major price of both our innocence and our control." (page 247)

Take turns, for one minute each, slowly reading the above quotation aloud to your partner. As your partner reads to you, notice which words or phrases stand out to you.

Then, take one minute to read over the quotation by yourself, reflecting on the emotions, physical sensations, thoughts, and memories that arise within you.

Take two minutes each to share something of these reflections with your partner. When it's your turn to listen, give your partner the gift of your presence.

**Solo Reflection:**
Take three minutes of quiet to individually reflect on aspects of the Pattern of Spiritual Transformation: Order, Disorder, Reorder (a summary is below, but you may wish to review the longer outline on pages 244–246):

> **Order**: "invariably operates from a worldview of scarcity and hardly ever from abundance."

> **Disorder**: "the 'fall' . . . is *necessary in some form* if any real growth is to occur; but some of us find this stage so uncomfortable we try to flee back to our first created order—even if it is killing us."

> **Reorder**: "It is an insistence on going *through—not under, over, or around*.... These wise ones have stopped overreacting but also overdefending. They are usually a minority of humans."

Reflect for three minutes on the following questions in your journal:

What has been your own personal experience of moving through Order, Disorder, and Reorder?

Which of these three—Order, Disorder, or Reorder—best describes your current experience?

What is life-giving, energizing, or hopeful about these experiences?

What is painful, tiring, or challenging about these experiences?

**Group Sharing (with Talking Stick):**
Using the talking stick, take turns sharing your reflections on any aspect of these questions with the group. Listen carefully to others as they speak and, when it is your turn, speak from the heart, sharing whatever is coming up for you at that moment. (Ten minutes total are allocated for this round of group sharing.)

Stay with your experience of listening to others. What distracts you? What makes you reactive? How can you stay present?

**Solo Reflection:**
Reflect for three minutes on the following quotation and question in your journal:

> "Conservatives must let go of their illusion that they can order and control the world through religion, money, war, or politics.... Liberals, however, must surrender their belief in permanent disorder, and their horror of all leadership, eldering, or authority, and find

what was good, healthy, and deeply true about a foundational order. This will normally be experienced as a move toward humility and real community." (page 246)

How has your experience in these group sessions allowed you to move toward humility and real community?

**FACILITATOR:**

***Thanks*** the group for their participation and invites each person to take the talking stick and share their thoughts on *any* of the following (twelve minutes total are allocated for this final round of group sharing):

How has the group interacted over the course of the eight sessions?

What kind of consciousness does the group now embody?

What effect has this had on you personally?

Stay with your experience of listening to others, whether they speak of challenges and difficulties or encouragements and hopes.

***Closes*** the group with the bell and invites people to leave in silence.

*Thank you very much for taking part in this group practice guide. We encourage you to look back over your notes, to journal, to reflect, and, most importantly, to continue with the spiritual practices that have resonated with you over these eight sessions.*

# ENGAGEMENT

## Group Guide

Welcome to this Engagement practice group for *The Universal Christ: How a Forgotten Reality Can Change Everything We See, Hope For, and Believe*, Fr. Richard Rohr's most important book to date. This Group Guide provides instructions for each practice group session. There will also be a facilitator for your group, who will explain the practices, keep time, guide group sharing, and answer questions you may have about the group process and practices.

Before the first gathering, please read and commit to the following.

**Agreements for Group Participation**

- Reading the book.
- Respecting the group guidelines and the role of the facilitator.
- No commenting or interrupting when a group member is sharing.
- Holding confidentiality throughout the course of the group sessions, inside and outside of the sessions.
- Sharing *only* one's own personal story.

**Modalities for Participation**
The Group Guide has been formulated in a way that allows for a balance of group work, pair sharing, and solo reflection:

- **Group Work** involves group sharing in a circle using a "talking stick" (introduced by the facilitator at the first session), reflective *Lectio* practice, and contemplative sit. It is a time to deepen into a felt sense of the mind and body of Christ.
- **Pair Sharing** will give individuals an opportunity to share what is true for them with one other person and to practice being an attentive listening presence to their partners.

- **Solo Reflection** is time for individuals to process the content as it relates to their own lives.

## Group Sharing Guidelines

- Gather in a circle.
- Use the talking stick.
- Speak in the moment (try not to prepare something in advance).
- Speak from the heart (speak what is *true* for you, regardless of whether it is "right").
- Be lean of speech (share a few sentences at most, with time to pause and ponder in between).
- Listen from the heart (respect the honest sharing of others and listen in a way that moves you beyond thinking of what this means to *you*; instead, what does this mean to the person who is sharing?).
- Respect confidentiality in this sacred space (what is shared in the group *must* stay in the group; otherwise the group cannot grow together).

In group sharing, be mindful of not speaking or commenting when individuals are sharing. Practicing presence, by not speaking too much and listening in silence, is an important part of group sessions. Each week, bring your copy of *The Universal Christ*, this Group Guide, a journal for recording your reflections, and a Bible to the session.

Before the first meeting, read chapters 1 and 2 of *The Universal Christ*.

# ENGAGEMENT

**WEEK I OF VIII**
**Chapters: 1 and 2**

**FACILITATOR:**

*Introduces* the first contemplative sit with the following quotation:

> "Every life has an influence on every other kind of life." (page 4)

*Reads* the text slowly and clearly for the whole group to hear.

*Rings* a prayer bell to indicate that the contemplative sit has begun. After eight minutes, the facilitator rings a prayer bell to indicate that the contemplative sit has finished.

**Solo Reflection:**
Take two minutes to read the quotation and reflect on the question in your journal.

> "If my own experience is any indication, the message in this book can transform the way you see and the way you live in your everyday world." (page 6)

What messages have had the most significant impact on how you see the world and the way you live in it?

**Pair Sharing:**
In pairs, share your response to the following quotation. (Allow two minutes for each person.)

> "We ended up spreading our national cultures under the rubric of Jesus, instead of a universally liberating message under the name of Christ." (page 18)

**Group Sharing (with Talking Stick):**
Take one minute to silently reflect on this quotation. Notice what arises in you as you read it (thoughts, feelings, sensations of resonance or dissonance):

> "But God loves things by becoming them.
> God loves things by uniting with them, not by excluding them." (page 16)

Your facilitator will review the Group Sharing Guidelines. Then you will take turns briefly sharing how this quotation impacted you on a personal level. Stay with your experience of listening to others, noting what distracts you, what makes you reactive, and how you stay present as an attentive listener. (Twelve minutes total are allocated for this round of group sharing.)

**Solo Reflection:**
Take two minutes to read this quotation and reflect on the questions in your journal.

> "The Christ Mystery anoints all physical matter with eternal purpose... first in creation; second in Jesus, 'so that we could hear him, see him with our eyes, watch him, and touch him with our hands'... and third, in the ongoing beloved community... which is slowly evolving throughout all of human history (Romans 8:18ff). We are still in the Flow." (page 20)

Which of the three revelations of the Christ Mystery has been the easiest way for you to connect with "the Flow"? What has influenced that ease?

Which of the three has been the most challenging way for you to connect with "the Flow"? What has influenced that challenge? Set an intention or prayer to let this group be an arena in which you can work on the revelation that is most challenging to you.

**Pair Sharing:**

In pairs, take one minute in silence to reflect on the contrasts between the following two quotations from chapter 2 and share with your partner for two minutes each on what arises for you.

Notice, energetically in your body, what it felt like to discuss these quotations. What word(s) would you offer to describe the experience?

> "As long as we keep God imprisoned in a retributive frame instead of a restorative frame, we really have no substantial good news; it is neither good nor new, but the same old tired story line of history. We pull God down to our level." (pages 28–29)

> "Building on 2 Peter 1:4, where the author says, 'He has given us something very great and wonderful . . . you are *able to share the divine nature!*' This is Christianity's core good news and only transformative message." (pages 27–28)

## *Lectio*

**FACILITATOR:**

**Reads** the text below for the *Lectio*, slowly and clearly for the whole group to hear. Group members may read along with the text or choose to close their eyes and simply listen.

> "The only thing [Jesus] excluded was exclusion itself." (page 34)

***Reads*** the passage slowly and clearly a second time. Each person allows the quotation to "wash over them," noticing which word or phrase stands out for them.

### Group Sharing (with Talking Stick):

After one minute of silence, one person picks up the talking stick and briefly shares the word or phrase that stood out for them. Then, going around in a circle, everyone takes a turn to briefly share the word or phrase that stood out for them. If anyone chooses not to share a word or phrase, they simply say "pass" and hand the talking stick to the next person. (Two minutes total are allocated for this round of group sharing.)

***Says*** "I need to stop excluding . . ." and allows a minute of silence.

***Invites*** each person to take the talking stick and share, beginning with the phrase, "I need to stop excluding . . . ." (Twelve minutes total are allocated for this round of group sharing.)

***Reads*** the passage one last time and the group sits in contemplative silence for two minutes, allowing the divine lesson to sink in and settle within their whole being.

### Solo Reflection:

In silence, take two minutes to reflect on the following question in your journal.

What is being asked of you right now?

**FACILITATOR:**

***Closes*** the group with the bell and invites people to leave in silence.

**Solo Reflection at Home (Optional):**

**Exercise 1**

Reflect in your journal on how you participated in the group and how that contributed to the experience of others within the group. (These reflections will not be shared with the group.)

**Exercise 2**

Practice a *Lectio* of your own on this text:

> *"You are a child of God, and always will be, even when you don't believe it. This is why [you can] see Christ . . . in those who do not like you, and those who are not like you."* (page 37)

**Exercise 3**

This week, as you encounter people that you do not naturally like, reflect in your journal on how you respond to them. *Can you see Christ in them?*

*Please read chapters 3 and 4 before our next meeting.*

# WEEK II OF VIII
## Chapters: 3 and 4

**FACILITATOR:**

*Invites* the group to begin with a contemplative sit for ten minutes, after reading the following quotation from chapter 3:

> "'There is only Christ. He is everything and he is in everything' (Colossians 3:11)." (pages 16–17)

## Solo Reflection:
Take one minute to read this quotation three times, pausing between each reading. Then take two minutes to write your response to the reflection in your journal.

> "*I have never been separate from God, nor can I be, except in my mind.*" (page 44)

What arises in your being? Describe your holistic experience (cognitive, emotional, physiological).

## Pair Sharing:
With a partner, take turns sharing your reflections on the following quotation for two minutes each:

> "I cannot help but think that future generations will label the first two thousand years of Christianity 'early Christianity.' They will, I believe, draw out more and more of the massive implications of this understanding of a Cosmic Christ." (page 48)

## Group Sharing (with Talking Stick):
Take two minutes to reflect in silence on this quotation. Notice what arises in you (thoughts, feelings, sensations of resonance or dissonance).

> "We would have helped history and individuals so much more if we had spent our time revealing how Christ is everywhere instead of proving that Jesus was God." (page 48)

**FACILITATOR:**

*Invites* each person to take the talking stick and share, in just a few sentences, on this question: How can you engage with an aspect of your community in a way that reveals that Christ is everywhere (could be family, friends, or neighbors; local, national, or global community)? (Fifteen minutes total are allocated for this round of group sharing.)

## Solo Reflection:
Take two minutes to read and reflect on this quotation and respond to the question in your journal.

> "*In God you do not include less and less; you always see and love more and more.* The more you transcend your small ego, the more you can include. 'Unless the single grain of wheat dies, it remains just a single grain. But if it does, it will bear much fruit,' Jesus Christ says (John 12:24)." (page 52)

To what are you being called to die right now in your life so that you can *"see and love more and more"*? What support do you have, or need to find, to go through this kind of death?

## Pair Sharing:
Take one minute to reflect on how you might have experienced the following in your own life:

> "For Paul and for ordinary mystics like you and me, the kind of seeing I'm describing is a relational and reciprocal experience, in which we find God simultaneously in ourselves and in the outer world

beyond ourselves. I doubt if there is any other way. Presence is never self-generated, but always a gift from another, and faith is always relational at the core . . . because you are already fully accepted and fully accepting." (pages 52–53)

Share with your partner for two minutes each about what is coming up for you right now. As you listen, practice the gift of being a fully accepting presence with your partner. End your sharing by bringing your hands together and offering a small bow to each other in recognition of the sacred nature of your relational and reciprocal experience.

**Solo Reflection:**
Take two minutes to read and reflect on these quotations. In what ways do you wish to bring faith, hope, and love into situations in your life right now, either internally or in community (again, this could be family, friends, or neighbors; local, national, or global community)?

> "In Catholic theology we called these three essential attitudes the 'theological virtues.' . . . In this understanding, faith, hope, and love are far more defining of the human person than the 'moral virtues,' the various good behaviors we learn as we grow older. This is why I cannot abandon an Orthodox or Catholic worldview. For all of their poor formulations, they still offer humanity a foundationally *positive anthropology*." (page 65)

> "But our saying yes to such implanted faith, hope, and love plays a crucial role in the divine equation; human freedom matters. . . . *we matter*." (pages 65–66)

**Group Sharing (with Talking Stick):**
Using the talking stick, take turns sharing with the group. Don't plan what you will say. Listen carefully to others as they speak. When it is your turn, speak from the heart, sharing whatever is coming up for

you at that very moment. (Fifteen minutes total are allocated for this round of group sharing.)

Facilitator closes the group with the bell and invites people to leave in silence.

**Solo Reflection at Home (Optional):**

**Exercise 1**

Reflect in your journal on how you participated in the group and how that contributed to the experience of others within the group.

**Exercise 2**

> "We have spent centuries trying to solve the 'problem' that we're told is at the heart of our humanity. But if you start with a problem, you tend to never get beyond that mind-set." (page 62)

Where are you just seeing problems at this time in your life?

Where are you seeing faith, hope, love, growth, and freedom at this time?

*Please read chapters 5, 6, and 7 before our next meeting.*

# WEEK III OF VIII
## Chapters: 5 through 7

*Lectio*

**FACILITATOR:**

**Welcomes** the group and invites everyone to observe a minute of silence by way of settling into their seats and feeling present to themselves and the rest of the group.

**States** that the text for the *Lectio* is from Teilhard de Chardin's *Divine Milieu* and reads the text slowly and clearly for the whole group to hear. Group members may read along with the text or choose to close their eyes and simply listen.

> "God does not offer Himself to our finite beings as a thing all complete and ready to be embraced. For us, He is eternal discovery and eternal growth. The more we think we understand Him, the more he reveals himself as otherwise. The more we think we hold him, the further He withdraws, drawing us into the depths of himself." (page 78)

**Reads** the passage slowly and clearly a second time. Each person allows the quotation to "wash over them," noticing which word or phrase stands out for them.

### Group Sharing (with Talking Stick):

After a minute of silence, one person picks up the talking stick and briefly shares the word or phrase that stood out for them. Then, going around in a circle, everyone takes a turn to briefly share the word or phrase that stood out for them. If anyone chooses not to share a word or phrase, they simply say "pass"' and hand the talking stick to the next person. (Two minutes total are allocated for this round of group sharing.)

**Solo Reflection:**
Take two minutes to read these quotations and reflect on the two questions in your journal.

> "The world was shocked to discover that Mother Teresa had many years of darkness and what looked to the secular world like depression. It was anything but." (page 78)

> "I must be honest with you here about my own life. For the last ten years I have had little spiritual 'feeling,' neither consolation nor desolation. Most days, I've had to simply choose to believe, to love, and to trust." (pages 78–79)

What were your initial reactions as you read about these experiences of Mother Teresa and Fr. Richard?

Reflecting on your life, right now, how are your experiences similar to and how are they different from those described above?

Take two minutes to read this quotation, mulling over it a number of times, then take a minute to write what it evokes for you.

> "But God rewards me for letting him reward me.
> This is the divine two-step that we call grace:
> I am doing it, and yet I am not doing it;
> It is being done unto me, and yet by me too.
> *Yet God always takes the lead in the dance, which we only recognize over time.*" (page 79)

**Pair Sharing:**
Take one minute to reflect in silence on how you might have experienced this in your own life.

"To complete the circuit of Divine Love, we often need a moment of awe, a person who evokes that electric conductivity, something we can deeply respect, or even call 'Father' or 'Mother' or 'Lover' or just 'beautiful.' Only then do we find the courage and confidence to complete God's circuit from our side. This is why people know they do not fully choose love; they fall into it, allow it, and then receive its strong charge. The evidence that you are involved in this flow will often seem two-sided. *You are simultaneously losing control and finding it.*" (pages 76–77)

Share with your partner for two minutes each about what is coming up for you right now. As you listen, practice the gift of being a fully accepting presence with your partner. End your sharing by bringing your hands together and offering a small bow to each other in recognition of the sacred nature of your relational and reciprocal experience.

### Group Sharing (with Talking Stick):

Take one minute to silently reflect on this quotation. Notice what arises in you as you read it (thoughts, feelings, sensations of resonance or dissonance):

> "'My pilgrim's progress has been to climb down a thousand ladders until I could finally reach out a hand of friendship to the little clod of earth that I am.'" —C. G. Jung (page 86)

**FACILITATOR:**

***Invites*** each person to take the talking stick and share their response to this question: What has been your experience of *"climbing down a thousand ladders"* on your pilgrim's progress? (Fifteen minutes total are allocated for this round of group sharing.)

Stay with your experience of listening to others. What distracts you, what makes you reactive, and how do you stay present as an attentive listener?

**Solo Reflection:**
Take five minutes to read this quotation and reflect on the questions in your journal.

> "How does anyone achieve such a holding together of opposites—things like inner acceptance and outer resistance, intense suffering and perfect freedom, my little self and an infinite God, sensuality and intense spirituality, the need to blame somebody and the freedom to blame nobody? . . . Christ [is] a universally available 'voice' that calls all things to *become whole and true to themselves*. God's two main tools in this direction, from every appearance, seem to be great love and great suffering—and often great love that *invariably leads* to great suffering." (page 83)

Reflect on a time in your life when you experienced great love or great suffering. What were the facts of that situation? (Separate the facts from the emotions you felt.)

Now reflect on the emotions you felt at that time. Looking back, can you feel/see any tension of opposites (e.g. "intense suffering and perfect freedom")?

Did this experience lead you to become more *"whole and true"* to yourself? If so, in what way(s)? If not, what effect did this experience have on you?

How does this experience influence you in the present moment as you reflect on it?

**Pair Sharing:**

> "*There is no such thing as a nonpolitical Christianity.* To refuse to critique the system of the status quo is to fully support it." (page 94)

In pairs, reflect for three minutes each on these questions.

Where have you been able to step back and see the systems at play, such as privilege, nationhood, or religion? (page 94)

How has your ego tried to hold you above these systems or apart from them? (page 94)

When you have both finished speaking, take one minute of silence to reflect on the following question in your journal:

What is being asked of you right now?

End by bringing your hands together and offering a small bow to each other in recognition of the sacred nature of the relational and reciprocal experience you just had.

**FACILITATOR:**

*Invites* the group to practice a contemplative sit. The preparatory text for the sit is a quote from chapter 7:

> "I am afraid many of us have failed to honor God's always unfolding future and the process of getting there, which usually includes some form of dying to the old." (page 93)

*Reads* the text slowly and clearly for the whole group to hear.

*Rings* a prayer bell to indicate that the contemplative sit has begun.

***Closes*** the group with the bell after twelve minutes and invites people to leave in silence.

**Solo Reflection at Home (Optional):**

**Exercise 1**

Leading in with the following quotation, practice another contemplative sit of your own this week. You may wish to set a timer or a prayer bell so that you know when to finish.

> "This point is worth sitting with for a few moments.
> *Every time you take in a breath, you are repeating the pattern of taking spirit into matter, and thus repeating the first creation of Adam.*
> *And every time you breathe out, you are repeating the pattern of returning spirit to the material universe.* In a way, every exhalation is a 'little dying' as we pay the price of inspiriting the world.
> Your simple breathing models your entire vocation as a human being. You are an incarnation, like Christ, of matter and spirit operating as one." (page 99)

If you wish, write down your reflections of your experience of this sit.

**Exercise 2**

> "As C. G. Jung inscribed over his doorway, *Vocatus atque non vocatus, Deus aderit*, 'Invoked or not invoked, God is still present.'" (page 100)

Write down "*Vocatus atque non vocatus, Deus aderit*" and keep it with you throughout this week.

Read it each morning and reflect on how you wish to engage in the world around you today. It may help to write some notes on this.

Read it each evening and reflect on how you engaged in the world around you during the day. Again, it may help to write some notes on this.

**Exercise 3**

> *"The Risen Christ is not a one-time miracle but the revelation of a universal pattern that is hard to see in the short run."* (page 100)

In what ways do you see traces of this *"universal pattern"* at play this week?

> *"God has worked anonymously since the very beginning—it has always been an inside and secret sort of job. The Spirit seems to work best underground. When aboveground, humans start fighting about it."* (page 100)

In what ways are you being asked to work underground at the moment?

In what ways are you being asked to work aboveground at the moment?

Energetically, what difference do these differing orientations make on how you engage with others?

*Please read chapters 8, 9, and 10 before our next meeting.*

## WEEK IV OF VIII
## Chapters: 8 through 10

**FACILITATOR:**

*Invites* the group to begin with a contemplative sit for five minutes, after reading the following quotation from chapter 9:

> "There must be a way to be both *here* and in the *depth of here*. Jesus is the here, Christ is the depth of here." (page 118)

### Solo Reflection:
Take three minutes to read this quotation and reflect on the questions in your journal.

> "Is our only mission to merely keep announcing our vision and philosophy statement? Sometimes it has seemed that way. This is what happens when power and empire take over the message." (page 105)

When has your expression of spirituality been more a "vision and philosophy statement" than anything else? What is it like to think and act in this way?

What is your spiritual experience now?

Take a moment to challenge yourself by reflecting on the ways "power and empire" might still affect your engagement in the world.

### Pair Sharing:

> "Throughout his life, Jesus himself spent no time climbing, but a lot of time descending, *'emptying himself and becoming as all humans are'* (Philippians 2:7), 'tempted in every way that we are' (Hebrews 4:15)

and 'living in the limitations of weakness' (Hebrews 5:2)." (pages 110–111)

Take one minute to reflect on how you have experienced both climbing and descending in your own life.

Then, share with your partner for two minutes each about what is coming up from your very depths right now. Again, as you listen, practice the gift of being a fully accepting presence with your partner.

When you have both finished speaking, take one minute of silence to reflect on the following questions in your journal:

What is being asked of you right now?

In what ways do you sense you are being invited to further engage in the path of descent?

End by bringing your hands together and offering a small bow to each other in recognition of the sacred nature of the relational and reciprocal experience you just had.

*Lectio*

**FACILITATOR:**

*Reads* the text below for the *Lectio*, slowly and clearly for the whole group to hear. Group members may read along with the text or choose to close their eyes and simply listen.

> "God hides in the depths and is not seen as long as we stay on the surface of anything—even the depths of our sins." (page 111)

*Reads* the passage slowly and clearly a second time. Each person allows the quotation to "wash over them," noticing which word or phrase stands out for them.

### Group Sharing (with Talking Stick):
After one minute of silence, one person picks up the talking stick and briefly shares the word or phrase that stood out for them. Then, going around in a circle, everyone takes a turn to briefly share the word or phrase that stood out for them. If anyone chooses not to share a word or phrase, they simply say "pass" and hand the talking stick to the next person. (Two minutes total are allocated for this round of group sharing.)

### Solo Reflection:
In silence, take one minute to linger over this word or phrase; "to focus on it until it engages your body, your heart, your awareness of the physical [and unseen] world around you." (page 8)

**FACILITATOR:**

*Invites* each person to take the talking stick and share, in a few sentences, the connection between the word or phrase and their life. (Twelve minutes total are allocated for this round of group sharing.)

*Reads* the passage one last time and the group sits in contemplative silence for five minutes, allowing the divine lesson to sink in and settle within their whole being.

### Solo Reflection:

Take two minutes to read this quotation and reflect on the two questions in your journal.

> "It's no stretch to say that the New Testament faith was, in effect, written by two men who profoundly relied upon their inner

experience of the ways of God despite a totally dominant consciousness that insisted otherwise. How did they get away with it? The answer is, in their lifetimes, they largely didn't. Only later did saints and scholars see that Jesus and Paul had drawn upon the deepest sources of their own tradition to then totally reframe that tradition for the larger world. They, like all the prophets, were 'radical traditionalists.' *You can only reform things long term by unlocking them from inside—by their own chosen authoritative sources.* Outsiders have little authority or ability to reform anything." (pages 116–117)

What is your first reaction upon reading this quotation?

Where are your opportunities as an insider to unlock things?

**Pair Sharing:**
In pairs, take five minutes total to reflect on the quotation and respond to the questions with your partner.

> "In Mary, we see that God must never be forced on us, and God never comes uninvited. If Christ and Jesus are the archetypes of what God is doing, Mary is the archetype of *how to receive what God is doing* and *hand it on to others.*" (page 127)

What is the role of community in your position as a receiver? Who are the "Marys" handing God to you?

Having received from God, how do you hand this on to others? What is the role of community in your position of handing it on?

As you listen, practice the gift of fully accepting presence with your partner. End by bringing your hands together and offering a small bow to each other in recognition of the sacred nature of the relational and reciprocal experience you just had.

**FACILITATOR:**

*Reads* the following quotation to the group:

> "Today on many levels, we are witnessing an immense longing for the mature feminine at every level of our society—from our politics, to our economics, in our psyche, our cultures, our patterns of leadership, and our theologies, all of which have become far too warlike, competitive, mechanistic, and noncontemplative. We are terribly imbalanced." (page 128)

*Guides* the group in a short practice based on the following quotation:

> "Like the Christ Mystery itself, *the deep feminine* often works underground and in the shadows, and—from that position—creates a much more intoxicating message. . . . Feminine power is deeply relational and symbolic—and thus transformative—in ways that men cannot control or even understand." (page 128)

*Reads* the text slowly and clearly for the whole group to hear. Group members may read along with the text or choose to close their eyes and simply listen. (This first reading is to help group members familiarize themselves with the quotation.)

*Reads* the text slowly and clearly a second time. Each person allows the quotation to "wash over them," noticing which word or phrase stands out for them.

*Reads* the following prompt and invites one minute of silent reflection: "'Underground and in the shadows' of my life. . . ."

*Invites* each person to take the talking stick and share, beginning with: "'Underground and in the shadows' of my life. . . ." People can pass if they do not feel like sharing. (Fifteen minutes total are allocated for this round of group sharing.)

**Reads** the passage one last time and invites the group to sit in contemplative silence for two minutes, allowing the divine lesson to sink in and settle within their whole being.

**Closes** the group with the bell and invites people to leave in silence.

**Solo Reflection at Home (Optional):**

**Exercise 1**

> "In Mary, humanity has said *our* eternal yes to God. A yes that cannot be undone. A corporate yes that overrides our many noes." (page 128)

Notice and note down in your journal the times and situations in your week where you are personally answering God or life with a no.

Notice and note down the times and situations in your week where you are participating in some kind of a systemic structure that is answering with a no (perhaps a structure that excludes people on the margins).

Where in your life is God drawing you into further engagement with an unfettered yes? Pray for this in a way that seems most fitting.

*Please read chapters 11 and 12 before our next meeting.*

# WEEK V OF VIII
## Chapters: 11 and 12

**FACILITATOR:**

*Reads* the following quotation:

> "Life is the destiny you are bound to refuse until you have consented to die."
> —W. H. Auden, "For the Time Being" (page 129)

*Invites* the group to get comfortable, take some deep breaths, let go of the stresses of the day, and sit in silence for five minutes. (The facilitator may choose to use a prayer bell to mark the opening and closing of this sit.)

*Reads* the quotation again, waits for another minute, then invites participants into solo reflection.

## Solo Reflection:
Spend two minutes pondering the quotation and questions in your journal.

> "But Jesus turned religion and history on their heads, inviting us to imagine that God would give *himself as food for us!*" (page 131)

Gently close your eyes and experience the internal sensation of having a body. Choose one part of your body—a hand, a foot, your mouth—and feel into all the sensations that exist there. What do you notice?

Now, having examined your own body, reflect on the above quotation and the idea that "God would give [*his very body*] *as food for us!*" Note down what arises for you as you consider this.

**Pair Sharing:**
With your partner, take two minutes each to share your sense of this "Big Crunch":

> "The Great Circle of Inclusion (the Trinity) is a centrifugal force that will finally pull everything back into itself—exactly as many physicists predict will happen to the universe the moment it finally stops expanding. They call it the 'Big Crunch,' and some even say it will take a nanosecond to happen. (Could this be a real description of the 'Second Coming of Christ'? Or the 'Final Judgment'? I think so.)" (page 137)

As you listen, practice the gift of fully accepting presence with your partner. End by bringing your hands together and offering a small bow to each other in recognition of the sacred nature of the relational and reciprocal experience you just had.

*Lectio*

**FACILITATOR:**

> "We are not just humans having a God experience. The Eucharist tells us that, in some mysterious way, we are God having a human experience!... Who we are in God is who we all are." (pages 137–138)

***Reads*** the text slowly and clearly for the whole group to hear. Group members may read along with the text or choose to close their eyes and simply listen. (This first reading is to help the group familiarize themselves with the quotation.)

***Reads*** the passage slowly and clearly a second time. Each person allows the quotation to "wash over them," noticing which word or phrase stands out for them.

**Group Sharing (with Talking Stick):**
After a few moments of silence, one person picks up the talking stick and briefly shares the word or phrase that stood out for them. Then, going around in a circle, everyone takes a turn to briefly share the word or phrase that stood out for them. If anyone chooses not to share a word or phrase, they simply say "pass'" and hand the talking stick to the next person. (Two minutes total are allocated for this round of group sharing.)

**Solo Reflection:**
In silence, take one minute to reflect on this word or phrase; focus on it to find God hidden in the depths, *"not seen as long as we stay on the surface of anything."* (page 111)

**FACILITATOR:**

*Invites* each person to take the talking stick and share, in just a few sentences, the connection between the word or phrase and their sense of calling and engagement with the world. (Fifteen minutes total are allocated for this round of group sharing.)

*Reads* the passage one last time. The group sits in contemplative silence for two minutes, allowing the *Lectio* to sink in and settle within their whole being.

**Solo Reflection:**

> "It *is not God who is violent. We are.*
> *It is not that God demands suffering of humans. We do.*
> *God does not need or want suffering—neither in Jesus nor in us."*
> (page 146)

Sit with this quotation for one minute, then spend a minute journaling anything that comes up for you.

**Pair Sharing:**
Take two minutes to read through the following quotation silently and notice what resonates with you.

> "Saints are those who wake up while in this world, instead of waiting for the next one. Francis of Assisi, William Wilberforce, Thérèse of Lisieux, and Harriet Tubman did not feel superior to anyone else; they just knew they had been let in on a big divine secret, and they wanted to do their part in revealing it. *They all refused to trust even their own power unless that power had first been taught and refined by powerlessness.*
>
> "This is no easy truth. Once their entire frame of mind had been taken apart and reshaped in this way, they had to figure out how they fit back into the dominant worldview—and most of them never did, at least not completely. This became their crucifixion. The 'way of the cross' can never go out of style because it will surely never be *in* style. It never becomes the dominant consciousness anywhere. But this is the powerlessness of God, the powerlessness that saves the world." (page 153)

Take four minutes each to share your responses to these questions:

What resonates with you?

What do you shy away from?

How does this relate to the manner in which you engage in the various aspects of your life in the world (as family, friend, or neighbor; local, national, or global citizen)?

As you listen, practice the gift of fully accepting presence with your partner. End by bringing your hands together and offering a small bow to each other in recognition of the sacred nature of the relational and reciprocal experience you just had.

**FACILITATOR:**

***Invites*** the group to end the session by practicing a contemplative sit and reads the following text slowly and clearly for the whole group to hear:

> "He did not come to change God's mind about us. It did not need changing. Jesus came to change our minds about God—and about ourselves—and about where goodness and evil really lie." (page 151)

***Rings*** a prayer bell to indicate that the contemplative sit has begun. After twelve minutes, the facilitator rings a prayer bell to indicate that the contemplative sit has finished, and the session has ended.

## Solo Reflection at Home (Optional):

### Exercise 1

> "What the medieval mystics said is true, *Crux probat omnia*—'The cross legitimizes/proves/uses everything.' *(Stay with this Christian maxim until it makes sense to you.)*" (page 158)

"Stay with this maxim" throughout the week and note in your journal anything that arises within you.

### Exercise 2

> "A Dialogue with the Crucified God"
>
> "Wait until you have an open, quiet, and solitary slot of time, then pray it out loud so your ears can hear your own words from your own mouth. In addition, I suggest that you place yourself before a tender image of the crucified Jesus that will allow you to both give and receive." (page 155)

Following the instructions above, read through "A Dialogue with the Crucified God" (pages 155–158) at some point this week. Journal anything that arises for you.

*Please read chapters 13, 14, and 15 before our next meeting.*

## WEEK VI OF VIII
## Chapters: 13 through 15

**FACILITATOR:**

*Welcomes* the group and invites everyone to a minute of silence by way of settling into their seats and feeling present to themselves and the rest of the group, then slowly reads the following:

> "Some mystics even go so far as to say that individual suffering doesn't exist at all—and that there is only one suffering, it is all the same, and it is all the suffering of God." (page 162)

*Lectio*

**FACILITATOR:**

*Reads* the following text for the *Lectio* slowly and clearly for the whole group to hear. Group members may read along with the text or choose to close their eyes and simply listen. (This first reading is to help the group familiarize themselves with the quotation.)

> "A Crucified God is the dramatic symbol of *the one suffering* that God fully enters into *with us*—much more than just *for us*." (page 162)

*Reads* the passage slowly and clearly a second time, inviting the group to allow the quotation to "wash over them," noticing which word or phrase stands out for them.

After a minute of silence, one person picks up the talking stick and briefly shares the word or phrase that stood out for them. Then, going around in a circle, everyone takes a turn to briefly share the word or phrase that stood out for them. If anyone chooses not to share a word or phrase, they simply say "pass" and hand the talking stick to the next person. (Two minutes total are allocated for this round of group sharing.)

**Solo Reflection:**
In silence, take one minute to reflect on this word or phrase; focus on it to find God hidden in the depths, *"not seen as long as we stay on the surface of anything."* (page 111)

**FACILITATOR:**

*Invites* each person in the group to take the talking stick and share, in just a few sentences, the connection between the word or phrase and their life. (Eight minutes total are allocated for this round of group sharing.)

*Reads* the passage one last time and the group sits in contemplative silence for three minutes, allowing the divine lesson to sink in and settle within their whole being.

**Solo Reflection:**
Take three minutes to read over this quotation and respond to the questions in your journal.

> "The only way out of deep sadness is to go *with it* and *through it*.... When I try to heroically do it alone, I slip into distractions, denials, and pretending—and *I do not learn suffering's softening lessons.*" (page 161)

When have you tried to go it alone? How did it go?

How has community supported *"suffering's softening lesson"* in your life?

What has it taught you about the value of community over going it alone?

**Pair Sharing:**
Spend one minute silently pondering the following quotations.

> "The Universal Christ is trying to communicate at the deepest intuitive level that there is only One Life, One Death, and One Suffering on this earth. . . . Call it reality." (page 166)

> "The Gospel, by contrast, is about learning to live and die *in and with* God. . . . *We are all saved in spite of our mistakes and in spite of ourselves. We are all caught up in the cosmic sweep of Divine grace and mercy.*" (page 166)

Take two minutes each to share what comes up for you. As you listen, practice the gift of fully accepting presence with your partner. End by bringing your hands together and offering a small bow to each other in recognition of the sacred nature of the relational and reciprocal experience you just had.

**Group Sharing (with Talking Stick):**

> "'*Resurrection*' *is another word for change, but particularly positive change—which we tend to see only in the long run. In the short run, it often just looks like death.* The Preface to the Catholic funeral liturgy says, 'Life is not ended, it is merely changed.'" (page 171)

> "But the vagaries and disappointments of life's journey eventually make you long for some overall direction, purpose, or goal beyond getting through another day." (page 171)

Take two minutes to reflect on these quotes in silence. Then use the talking stick to share your thoughts with the group. (Ten minutes total are allocated for this round of group sharing.)

Don't plan what you will say. Listen carefully to others as they speak and, when it is your turn, speak from the heart, sharing whatever is coming up for you at that very moment. Stay with your experience of listening to others. What distracts you, what makes you reactive, and how do you stay present as an attentive listener?

**Solo Reflection:**
Spend three minutes pondering these quotations and reflections in your journal.

> "The resurrection of Jesus . . . might be better described as Jesus's 'universalization,' sort of an Einsteinian warping of time and space, if you will. Jesus was always objectively the Universal Christ, but now his significance for humanity and for us was made *ubiquitous, personal, and attractive* for those willing to meet Reality through him. Many do meet Divine Reality without this shortcut, and we must be honest about that." (page 178)

> "If death is not possible for the Christ, then it is not possible for anything that 'shares in the divine nature' (2 Peter 1:4). God is by definition eternal, and God is Love (1 John 4:16), which is also eternal (1 Corinthians 13:13), and this same Love has been planted in our hearts (Romans 5:5, 8:9) by the Spirit dwelling within us. *Such fully Implanted Love cannot help but evolve and prove victorious, and our word for that final victory is 'resurrection.'*" (pages 179–180)

Choosing one or both of the above quotations, write down anything that resonates with you and why.

Now, having done this, how do you feel? What impact does reflecting on ideas such as these have on your state of being?

**Pair Sharing:**
Take one minute in silence to reflect on the following quotations.

> "Mary Magdalene serves as a witness to personal love and intimacy, which for most people is the best and easiest start on the path toward universal love. Then in the garden at Easter, she experienced a sudden shift of recognition toward the universal Presence of Christ." (page 194)

> "[Paul] starts with the Universal Christ, which then leads him to a deep devotion to the crucified and resurrected Jesus. God can use either path as long as we stay on that path for the whole journey." (page 194)

Take two minutes each to respond to the following questions.

Which path do you personally resonate with the most: that of Mary Magdalene (from knowing Jesus to knowing the Universal Christ) or that of Paul (from knowing the Universal Christ to knowing Jesus)?

What life events and experiences have influenced this for you?

As you listen, practice the gift of fully accepting presence with your partner. End by bringing your hands together and offering a small bow to each other in recognition of the sacred nature of the relational and reciprocal experience you just had.

**Group Sharing (with Talking Stick):**
Take two minutes to reflect in silence on these passages:

> "In his thinking, we were supposed to live inside of an alternative society, almost a utopia, and from such fullness go out to 'the world.' Instead, we created a model whereby people live almost entirely in the world, fully invested in its attitudes toward money, war, power, and gender—and sometimes 'go to church.' I am not sure this is working!" (page 200)

"People like the Amish, the Bruderhof, Black churches, and members of some Catholic religious Orders probably have a better chance of actually maintaining an alternative consciousness, but most of the rest of us end up thinking and operating pretty much like our surrounding culture. Surely foreseeing this, Paul intended that his new people 'live in the church,' as it were—and from that solid base go out to the world. We still have it all backward, living fully in the worldly systems and occasionally going to church." (page 200)

Use the talking stick to share your thoughts on the following with the group (Twelve minutes total are allocated for this round of group sharing):

Have you ever had an experience of living inside an alternative community or has your experience been more like "sometimes go[ing] to church"?

Briefly describe your past experiences of community as well as the type of community experience you would like to co-create with others.

Listen carefully to others as they speak and, when it is your turn, speak from the heart, sharing whatever is coming up for you in that moment. Stay with your experience of listening to others. What distracts you, what makes you reactive, and how do you stay present as an attentive listener?

Facilitator closes the group with the bell and invites people to leave in silence.

## Solo Reflection at Home (Optional):

## Exercise 1

> "But remember, *the greater light you are, the greater shadow you cast.* And Paul is a huge light." (page 197)

As you discover more about yourself, your consciousness, and your spirituality, what kind of a shadow are you casting on your community (family, friends, and neighbors; national and global community)?

If you are uncertain about your shadow, ask one or two people who know you very well. (Even if you are fairly certain, it still might be an interesting exercise!)

What is your gut reaction to this idea of asking others to share their experiences of your shadow with you?

## Exercise 2

> "[Paul] would have agreed with Jesus, I think, that humans are punished *by* their sins more than *for* their sins." (page 196)

Use this quotation as an introduction to a sit this week.

You may also want to record your thoughts on this notion "that humans are punished *by* their sins more than *for* their sins." What is your own experience of this?

*Please read chapters 16, 17, and the Afterword before our next meeting.*

## WEEK VII OF VIII
Chapters: 16, 17, and Afterword

**FACILITATOR:**

*Invites* the group to begin with a contemplative sit for three minutes, after reading the following quotation:

> "The contemplative mind can see things in their depth and in their wholeness instead of just in parts. The binary mind, so good for rational thinking, finds itself totally out of its league in dealing with things like love, death, suffering, infinity, God, sexuality, or mystery in general. It just keeps limiting reality to two alternatives and thinks it is smart because it chooses one! . . . It is not our metaphysics ('what is real') that is changing, but our epistemology—*how we think we know what is real*." (page 205)

### Solo Reflection:
Spend five minutes pondering these quotations and questions in your journal.

> "Every world religion—*at the mature levels*—discovers some forms of practice to free us from our addictive mind, which we take as normal." (page 209)

Reflecting on your current practice, note down your experience of how it frees you from your addictive mind.

When does your addictive mind still take control in your life? Is your practice adequate to support you?

> "When Western civilization set out on its many paths of winning, accomplishment, and conquest, the contemplative mind seemed uninteresting or even counterproductive to our egoic purposes.

The contemplative mind got in the way of our left-brain philosophy of progress, science, and development, which were very good and necessary in their own way—*but not for soul knowledge.*" (page 210)

Can you sense a tension between Western civilization's sense of "progress" and contemplative "presence"? How might that tension be resolved?

**Pair Sharing:**
Begin by silently reading through the quotations and questions below.

> "In her book *Joy Unspeakable,* Barbara Holmes shows us how the Black and slave experience led to a very different understanding of the contemplative mind. She calls it 'crisis contemplation.' . . . Barbara teaches how the Black experience of moaning together, singing spirituals that lead to intense inner awareness, participating in de facto liturgies of lamentation, and engaging in nonviolent resistance produced a qualitatively different—but profound—contemplative mind that we saw in people like Fannie Lou Hamer, Harriet Tubman, Martin Luther King Jr., Howard Thurman, and Sojourner Truth." (pages 214–215)

> "Then there are the walking meditators . . . who teach the deep wisdom of goalless walking or 'living life at three miles an hour.' . . . Many others come to the contemplative mind through activities like music, dancing, and running. It is largely a matter of your inner goal and intention, and whatever quiets you in body, mind, and heart." (page 215)

> "Contemplation allows us to *see* things in their wholeness, and thus with respect (remember, *re-spect* means to see a second time)." (page 215)

After two minutes of reflection, take turns responding to the following questions (allow five minutes for each partner to share):

Aside from the exercises we have practiced throughout these sessions together, what other approaches to contemplation have had an impact on you?

What is the value of community in your contemplative practice(s)?

How does your practice intersect with your day-to-day life?

As you listen, practice the gift of fully accepting presence with your partner.

**Group Sharing (with Talking Stick):**

**FACILITATOR:**

*Reminds* the group to use the talking stick to share their reflections with the group.

*Invites* members to read the quotation below.

> "Suffering is seen as *the practical and real price for letting go of illusion, false desire, superiority, and separateness.* Suffering is also pointed out as the price we pay for *not* letting go, which might be an even better way to teach about suffering." (page 217)

Take a minute to sit with the above quotation and sense some of your own suffering. Using the talking stick, take turns sharing with the group on how you might be hanging on to "*illusion, false desire, superiority, or separateness.*" (Ten minutes total are allocated for this round of group sharing.)

Listen carefully to others as they speak and, when it is your turn, speak from the heart, sharing whatever is coming up for you in that moment. Stay with your experience of listening to others. What distracts you, what makes you reactive, how do you stay present as an attentive listener?

**Solo Reflection:**
Take five minutes to read over this poem more than once and respond to the questions in your journal.

### LOVE AFTER LOVE

*The time will come
when, with elation,
you will greet yourself arriving
at your own door, in your own mirror,
and each will smile at the other's welcome,*

*and say, sit here. Eat.
You will love again the stranger who was yourself.
Give wine. Give bread. Give back your heart
to itself, to the stranger who has loved you*

*all your life, whom you ignored
for another, who knows you by heart.
Take down the love letters from the bookshelf,
the photographs, the desperate notes,
peel your own image from the mirror.
Sit. Feast on your life.*

—Derek Walcott (page 234)

What is evoked from deep within you?

What line or lines strike you the most?

Describe the *"stranger who has loved you . . . who knows you by heart."* (Even with just a word or two—the first words that come to you.)

**Pair Sharing:**

One partner slowly reads Practice I on page 224 to the other (allow five minutes for each reading).

Once you have finished reading, give your partner a minute to return their full presence to the room.

Invite your partner, if they wish, to jot down any notes or reflections they might have.

Once they are finished writing, switch roles and repeat the process.

**Group Sharing (with Talking Stick):**

**FACILITATOR:**

*Invites* the group to get comfortable in their seats, to ground themselves in their bodies, and to take a few quiet, deep breaths as they wait for the reading to begin.

*Reads* aloud "The Divine Mirror" from pages 226–229.

*Gives* the group an opportunity to engage for five minutes total in a *brief* round of sharing, using the following question:

"What is evoked from deep within you in this moment?" (The facilitator may want to repeat this question as the talking stick is passed around.)

Stay with your experience of listening to others. What distracts you, what makes you reactive, and how do you stay present as an attentive listener?

*Closes* the group with the bell and invites people to leave in silence.

**Solo Reflection at Home (Optional):**

**Exercise 1**

Choosing either Practice I (beginning on page 224) or Practice II (beginning on page 225), take some solo time to repeat this practice during the week.

What is evoked within you now as you return to this practice on your own?

Where can you experience the divine mirror and where are you unable to experience it yet?

**Exercise 2**

Read through the poem "Love After Love" (page 234) a few times and notice which words, phrases, or images stand out for you now.

What emotions are you aware of as you reflect?

What does *"Take down the love letters form the bookshelf"* mean to you in this reading?

If God were to tell you to *"peel your own image from the mirror. Sit. Feast on your life"* today, what would that mean to you?

How can you, through your words and your presence, engage in a way that brings a similar message to those around you?

## Exercise 3

"In our Living School here in New Mexico we teach a methodology that we call our 'tricycle.' It moves forward on three wheels: *Experience, Scripture, and Tradition*, which must be allowed to regulate and balance one another. Very few Christians were given permission, or training, in riding all three wheels together, much less allowing experience to be the front wheel. We also *try to ride all three wheels in a 'rational' way,* knowing that if we give reason its own wheel, it will end up driving the whole car." (page 213)

What has been your experience of this "tricycle" of *"Experience, Scripture, and Tradition"* during the formative years of your faith/spiritual practice?

What is your experience of this "tricycle" now? What is influencing that experience?

What could you do to engage others in this "tricycle"?

## Exercise 4

"You discover a Larger Self underneath. You decide not to push yourself to the front of the line, and something much better happens in the back of the line. You let go of your narcissistic anger, and you find that you start feeling much happier. You surrender your need to control your partner, and finally the relationship blossoms. Yet each time it is a choice—and each time it is a kind of dying." (pages 218–219)

Using this quotation as a lead-in, practice a contemplative sit of your own at some point during the week. Take a few moments to read the passage first, then settle yourself into your seat and slowly read the same quotation out loud. You may wish to set a timer or a prayer bell so that you know when to finish.

**Exercise 5**

> "If Christ represents the resurrected state, then Jesus represents the crucified/resurrecting path of getting there. If Christ is the source and goal, then Jesus is the path from that source toward the goal of divine unity with all things." (page 216)

Read the above quotation as an introduction to your own contemplative sit.

A day later, read the same quotation in a *Lectio* manner, allowing the words and ideas to become a part of you.

*Please read the Appendixes before our next meeting.*

# WEEK VIII OF VIII
## Appendixes

**FACILITATOR:**

*Invites* the group to begin with a contemplative sit for five minutes, after reading the following quotation from Appendix II:

> "There is a crack in everything, that's how the light gets in."
> —Leonard Cohen (page 244)

## Solo Reflection:
Reflect on the following summaries of each of The Four Worldviews (as outlined in Appendix I) and then answer the questions in your journal (ten minutes are allocated for this reflection):

> The *material worldview* believes "that the outer, visible universe is the ultimate and 'real' world. People of this worldview have given us science, engineering, medicine, and much of what we now call 'civilization.'. . . A material worldview tends to create highly consumer-oriented and competitive cultures, which are often preoccupied with scarcity, since material goods are always limited." (page 238)

> "The *spiritual worldview* characterizes many forms of religion and some idealistic philosophies that recognize the primacy and finality of spirit, consciousness, the invisible world behind all manifestations. . . . But taken too far it can become ethereal and disembodied, disregarding ordinary human needs and denying the need for good psychology, anthropology, or societal issues of peace and justice. The spiritual worldview, taken too seriously, has little concern for the earth, the neighbor, or justice, because it considers this world largely as an illusion." (page 238)

"Those holding ... the *priestly worldview* are generally sophisticated, trained, and experienced people and traditions that feel their job is to help us put matter and Spirit together. They are the holders of the law, the scriptures, and the rituals; they include gurus, ministers, therapists, and sacred communities. People of the priestly worldview help us make good connections that are not always obvious between the material and spiritual worlds.... this view assumes that the two worlds are actually separate and need someone to bind them back together.... It describes what most of us think of as organized religion and much of the self-help world." (pages 238–239)

"The *incarnational worldview,* [is one] in which matter and Spirit are understood to have never been separate. Matter and spirit reveal and manifest each other. *This view relies more on awakening than joining, more on seeing than obeying, more on growth in consciousness and love than on clergy, experts, morality, scriptures, or rituals. The code word I am using in this entire book for this worldview is simply 'Christ.'* ... In Christian history, we see the *incarnational worldview* most strongly in the early Eastern Fathers, Celtic spirituality, many mystics who combined prayer with intense social involvement, Franciscanism in general, many nature mystics, and contemporary ecospirituality." (page 239)

What resonates with you from each of these worldviews?

What do you resist from each of these worldviews?

How does your experience of reading this book and/or participating in this group relate to each of these worldviews?

What changes have taken place within you as a result of your participation?

**Pair Sharing:**
With your partner, take five minutes each to share your answers to the above questions (from the Solo Reflection section). Feel free to share as much or as little as you feel comfortable sharing. As you listen, practice the gift of fully accepting presence with your partner.

**Group Sharing (with Talking Stick):**

> "The incarnational worldview grounds Christian holiness in objective and ontological reality instead of just moral behavior." (page 240)

> "We all come to wisdom at the major price of both our innocence and our control." (page 247)

Using one or both of the above quotations as a springboard, what do you now want to say to the group? Notice anything that is ready to burst forth. Using the talking stick, take turns to share your reflections with the group. (Twelve minutes total are allocated for this round of group sharing.)

You may want to journal what you notice.

Group Sharing will now continue through practicing the spiritual discipline of silence (in order to honor the transitions we make from Disorder to Reorder, when changes take place within us that move beyond words).

When it is your turn to take the talking stick, hold it and silently process/communicate with the group in a nonverbal way. Notice what it's like to engage with others from the heart, without using words.

As we give this opportunity to each other, become aware of the quality of presence that we offer one another. Notice what distracts you, what makes you reactive, and how you manage to stay present. (Six minutes total are allocated for this round of group sharing.)

**FACILITATOR:**

*Thanks* the group for their silent sharing and invites each person to take the talking stick and share their thoughts on *any* of the following (twelve minutes total are allocated for this final round of group sharing):

How has the group interacted over the course of the eight sessions?

What kind of consciousness does the group now embody?

What effect has this had on you personally?

How do you now feel compelled to engage in the world?

Stay with your experience of listening to others, whether they speak of challenges and difficulties or encouragements and hopes.

**FACILITATOR:**

*Invites* the group to close with a contemplative sit and rings the bell. (Five minutes are allocated for this sit.)

*Closes* the group with the bell and invites people to leave in silence.

**Solo Reflection at Home (Optional):**

**Exercise 1**

Having read *The Universal Christ* and experienced these group sessions, how does this impact your engagement in the world?

Moving forward, of what will you do more and of what will you do less?

## Exercise 2

> "If Christ represents the resurrected state, then Jesus represents the crucified/resurrecting path of getting there. If Christ is the source and goal, then Jesus is the path from that source toward the goal of divine unity with all things." (page 216)

Read the above quotation, allowing the words and ideas to become a part of you, as an introduction to your own contemplative sit.

*Thank you very much for taking part in this group practice guide. We encourage you to look back over your notes, to journal, to reflect, and, most importantly, to continue with the spiritual practices that have resonated with you over these eight sessions.*

# FACILITATOR GUIDE

# General Overview

Thank you for your willingness to facilitate a practice group for *The Universal Christ*, Fr. Richard Rohr's most important book to date. This Facilitator Guide will help you prepare for the practice group sessions.

The role of facilitator is essential to the health and effectiveness of the practice group. While the facilitator does not participate in the group practices, s/he is responsible for setting a hospitable, organized, and calming tone, together with keeping the group on track. This will come with its own growth opportunities and reasons to celebrate, so you are encouraged to engage with a person or community who will support you and pray for you throughout your time as a facilitator.

**Practical Considerations**
The size of your practice group should be between eight and twelve members, not including the facilitator.

The facilitator will need to have on hand at each meeting:

- bell or gong,
- candle,
- Bible,
- *The Universal Christ* book, and
- Group Guide.

Each week, the facilitator will need to:

- organize the group logistics, including room setup;
- do the required reading in *The Universal Christ*;
- review the week's material in the Group Guide and note the amount of time needed for each practice (these

numbers will change each week, depending on the number of elements);
- introduce and explain each practice during the group session;
- be the timekeeper for each practice;
- monitor the group sharing and ensure that it follows the guidelines established in the Group Guide; and
- be the contact point for questions or concerns throughout the course of the sessions.

**The Group Guide Structure**
The Group Guide has been formulated in a way that allows for a balance of group work, pair sharing, and solo reflection:

**Group Work** involves group sharing in a circle using a "talking stick," * reflective *Lectio* practice, and contemplative sit. It is a time to deepen into a felt sense of the mind and body of Christ.

> *The "talking stick" is introduced by the facilitator at the first session. It can consist of something as simple as an actual stick, a stone, or a paperweight. During group sharing, individuals pass around the talking stick and take turns sharing; only the one holding the talking stick speaks.

**Pair Sharing** will give individuals an opportunity to share what is true for them with one other person and to practice being an attentive listening presence to their partners.

**Solo Reflection** is time for individuals to process the content as it relates to their own lives.

**Time**
Allow 90 minutes for the first session. Subsequent sessions are designed to take no more than 60 minutes per session. It is important to respect both the facilitator's time and that of the group members.

### The Spiritual Discipline of an Experiential/Embodied Group

The purpose of the Group Guide is to facilitate a sequence of practices in which a group can engage together. The goal is for group members to contemplate more deeply on the content of the book, rather than using the book itself for group discussion.

### Using the Group Guide

The Group Guide is designed to be reused by multiple groups over time, with group members using their own journals to record reflections. You may wish to purchase a set of Group Guides, issue them to participants, and then collect them when that group has finished. If you do this, remind participants not to write in the Group Guide, since it is not theirs to keep.

The role of the facilitator is to keep the group on task, transition the group from one activity to another, and discourage the group from engaging in discussion and debate. The facilitator introduces the embodied spiritual practices, facilitates contemplative sit and *Lectio*, and guides the group in the use of the talking stick as part of group sharing.

The first session is particularly important, as it will set the tone for how the rest of the group sessions will be facilitated. The facilitator is strongly encouraged to follow the scripted text in the Group Guide, as the group will also have access to these scripts. Following the script is especially important if the group is relatively new to engaging in these types of spiritual practices.

### The First Group Session

At the start of the first group session, the facilitator:

- welcomes the group;
- shares a little about him/herself and why s/he is personally motivated to facilitate this group;

- communicates the number of weeks/sessions, the start and end times of each session, and any comments on the location of each session;
- reminds group members to bring their copy of *The Universal Christ*, this Group Guide, a journal, and a Bible each week;
- describes the group focus (i.e., moving away from *discussion and debate* toward *embodied, spiritual practices*);
- explains the types of exercises included in the Group Guide: Group Sharing (including contemplative sit, *Lectio*, and the use of a talking stick), Pair Sharing (including changing partners each week), and Solo Reflection; and
- outlines the agreements for group participation:

  ▷ Reading the book.
  ▷ Respecting the group guidelines and the role of the facilitator.
  ▷ No commenting or interrupting when a group member is sharing.
  ▷ Holding confidentiality throughout the course of the group sessions, inside and outside the sessions.
  ▷ Sharing *only* one's own personal story.

**Three Types of Reflection**

The Group Guide has been divided into the following three types of reflection practices:

**1. Solo Reflection**

During solo reflection, individuals reflect on their own. The group members may move from their seats, as long as they remain within the meeting room/space. The solo reflection exercise is timed (e.g., from one to five minutes). When appropriate, the facilitator can give the group a one-minute notice, so members have an opportunity to conclude their reflection.

## 2. Pair Sharing

In pair sharing, individuals meet with a partner. Individuals are asked to change partners each week, to avoid sharing with the same partner throughout the course of the weekly group sessions. The facilitator explains some benefits of sharing with a different partner each week (taking the risk of getting to know and be vulnerable with other people, being exposed to different perspectives and experiences). The facilitator will give pairs notice when half the sharing time is up, so that each person has time to both share and listen.

## 3. Group Work

Group work will include group sharing with the use of a talking stick, *Lectio*, and contemplative sits. These are forms of communal spiritual practices—a sacred way of interacting in community that emphasizes active listening to oneself and to others, rather than engaging in cognitive discourse.

### Group Sharing

As facilitator, you will need to notice and guide the energy and the pacing of the group as a whole.

The facilitator will note these Group Sharing guidelines in the first session, and elsewhere as needed (they are also found in the Group Guide):

### Group Sharing Guidelines

- Gather in a circle.
- Use the talking stick.
- Speak in the moment (try not to prepare something in advance).
- Speak from the heart (speak what is *true* for you, regardless of whether it is "right").

- Be lean of speech (share a few sentences at most, with time to pause and ponder in between).
- Listen from the heart (respect the honest sharing of others and listen in a way that moves you beyond thinking of what this means to *you*; instead, what does this mean to the person who is sharing?).
- Respect confidentiality in this sacred space (what is shared in the group *must* stay in the group; otherwise the group cannot grow together).

In group sharing, be mindful of not speaking or commenting when individuals are sharing. Practicing patience, by not speaking too much and listening in silence, is an important part of group sessions.

## Lectio

*Lectio* is a practice of reading, meditating on, and praying with Scripture and/or other spiritually based source material.

Read the text in advance of a session, so as to be familiar with the content. You may wish to spend some time engaging in a *Lectio* of your own, using the text, as part of your preparation for the group session. This will give you a general sense of the timing and cadences of the *Lectio* that you will lead.

Review the instruction for group sharing and calculate the time it will take for the *Lectio* practice, predicated on the number of group participants. (If there are ten members in the group, and there are 15 minutes allotted for the *Lectio* practice, 1–1.5 minutes\* of reflection per person is appropriate.)

> \*Silent pauses are particularly important between reflections throughout the *Lectio* practices. (The speed at which you read and speak will guide, and affect, the experience of the group.)

Some group members may have never engaged in *Lectio* like this before, so it is important to ease their concerns at the start. If necessary, answer a question or two, then simply invite them to *experience* the practice, regardless of any concerns they may have.

> Note: If you think it would be helpful, you may want to talk about your own experience of Lectio *practice. If you do share, be concise and speak from the heart.*

If the group struggles through the *Lectio* practice, remind them that *Lectio* is an invitation to move deeper through reflection, meditation, and prayer, so as to avoid discussion or analysis.

## Contemplative Sit

Contemplative sit may be new to some members of the group. Familiarize yourself with the scripted text in the Group Guide ahead of time. Review the instructions with the group and determine the contemplative sit time in advance (suggested times will be given for each week, depending on the number of elements).

Prepare the room ahead of time with a lighted candle and a prayer bell to gently indicate the start and end of the contemplative sit.

> Note: You may wish to use a digital prayer bell from your cell phone or tablet meditation app.

Explain to the group the use of a sacred word, such as Yah-weh or Je-sus, or simply invite them to focus on their breath—in and out—whenever distracting thoughts enter their minds, so as to bring them back to the present moment.

Some group members, who may have never engaged in contemplative sit, could struggle with the practice initially, so simply invite them to allow themselves to *experience* the practice, using the following script:

As we begin our sit, let's take a few moments to notice our posture. Becoming comfortable in our seat, let's sit slightly forward, so that our spine is no longer touching the back of the seat. (Pause) Let's become aware of both of our feet touching the floor, grounding us in the present moment. (Pause) Let's focus on our back and our neck, allowing them to find their most aligned and neutral positions. (Pause) Now, I invite us to lower our gaze and focus on a point on the floor in front of us. Or, if we feel comfortable, we may want to close our eyes. (Pause)

As we begin our contemplation, let's remember that we are not trying to "achieve" anything. (Pause) There are no goals. (Pause) We are simply becoming aware of this moment. (Pause) Becoming aware of our presence in this moment. (Pause) Noticing any distractions, thoughts, judgments, decisions, ideas that cross our mind, we choose to let them go for now (Pause) and to focus instead on our moment-by-moment experience of being present to What Is. (Pause) God's Presence (Pause); the Larger Field (Pause); *en Cristo* (Pause). As we become distracted, frustrated, or confused, we consciously return to offering up our moment-by-moment presence to God's Presence by using a sacred word or simply focusing on our breath. (Pause) We know that God's Presence is already within us, whether we're aware of it or not. (Pause) No offering up is needed—we are offering in. (Pause) Into the silence. (Pause) Into each moment that we sit in contemplation. (Pause)

*Note: If you think it would be helpful, you may want to share your own experience of contemplative sit. If you do share, be concise and speak from the heart.*

## Optional Practices for Solo Reflection at Home
There are *optional* weekly solo practices following each session. Many of these exercises are designed to be kept completely private and

some of these exercises are suitable for sharing with others. However, due to time constraints, material from these solo reflections will not be shared during the group sessions. If individuals wish to share about their solo reflections, they must do so on their own time, outside the group sessions. Confidentiality must be observed, both within and outside the group sessions.

*Thank you again for choosing to be a facilitator. This role requires a significant commitment of your time and energy. We wish you a rich and peaceful experience with your group.*

Center for
Action and
Contemplation

A collision of opposites forms the cross of Christ.
One leads downward preferring the truth of the humble.
The other moves leftward against the grain.
But all are wrapped safely inside a hidden harmony:
One world, God's cosmos, a benevolent universe.